The Easy 5-Ingredient Meal Prep Cookbook

The Easy 5-Ingredient MEAL PREP Cookbook

Meal Plans and Recipes to Save Time

Michelle Anderson

Photography by Hélène Dujardin

ROCKRIDGE PRESS

As always, to my family, Scott, Mac, and Cooper, who inspire me to do better and who are an endless source of pride and joy. Even when they need me to find things when I am neck-deep in bread dough or trying to finish an important paragraph.

Copyright © 2020 by Rockridge Press, Emeryville, California

No part of this publication may be reproduced, stored in a retrieval system, or transmitted in any form or by any means, electronic, mechanical, photocopying, recording, scanning, or otherwise, except as permitted under Sections 107 or 108 of the 1976 United States Copyright Act, without the prior written permission of the Publisher. Requests to the Publisher for permission should be addressed to the Permissions Department, Rockridge Press, 6005 Shellmound Street, Suite 175, Emeryville, CA 94608.

Limit of Liability/Disclaimer of Warranty: The Publisher and the author make no representations or warranties with respect to the accuracy or completeness of the contents of this work and specifically disclaim all warranties, including without limitation warranties of fitness for a particular purpose. No warranty may be created or extended by sales or promotional materials. The advice and strategies contained herein may not be suitable for every situation. This work is sold with the understanding that the Publisher is not engaged in rendering medical, legal, or other professional advice or services. If professional assistance is required, the services of a competent professional person should be sought. Neither the Publisher nor the author shall be liable for damages arising herefrom. The fact that an individual, organization, or website is referred to in this work as a citation and/or potential source of further information does not mean that the author or the Publisher endorses the information the individual, organization, or website may provide or recommendations they/it may make. Further, readers should be aware that websites listed in this work may have changed or disappeared between when this work was written and when it is read.

For general information on our other products and services or to obtain technical support, please contact our Customer Care Department within the United States at (866) 744-2665, or outside the United States at (510) 253-0500.

Rockridge Press publishes its books in a variety of electronic and print formats. Some content that appears in print may not be available in electronic books, and vice versa.

TRADEMARKS: Rockridge Press and the Rockridge Press logo are trademarks or registered trademarks of Callisto Media Inc. and/or its affiliates, in the United States and other countries, and may not be used without written permission. All other trademarks are the property of their respective owners. Rockridge Press is not associated with any product or vendor mentioned in this book.

Interior and Cover Designer: Sean Doyle
Art Producer: Tom Hood
Editor: Myryah Irby
Production Editor: Emily Sheehan
Photography by Hélène Dujardin, © 2020
Food styling by Anna Hampton

ISBN: Print 978-1-64611-585-3 | eBook 978-1-64611-586-0
R0

Contents

Introduction vii

PART I: SIMPLIFYING MEAL PREP 1

CHAPTER 1: Week 1 Prep 11

CHAPTER 2: Week 2 Prep 21

CHAPTER 3: Week 3 Prep 31

CHAPTER 4: Week 4 Prep 41

CHAPTER 5: Week 5 Prep 51

CHAPTER 6: Week 6 Prep 61

CHAPTER 7: Week 7 Prep 71

CHAPTER 8: Week 8 Prep 81

CHAPTER 9: Week 9 Prep 91

CHAPTER 10: Week 10 Prep 101

CHAPTER 11: Week 11 Prep 111

CHAPTER 12: Week 12 Prep 121

PART II: BONUS MEAL PREP RECIPES 131

CHAPTER 13: Breakfast 133

CHAPTER 14: Lunch and Dinner 145

CHAPTER 15: Snacks and Sweets 159

CHAPTER 16: Seasonings, Dressings, and Sauces 171

Measurement Conversions 181

Index 182

Introduction

Food is one of life's pleasures. It is the anchor of joyful events, a comfort when you need a lift, and nourishment for your body so you can be your best at all stages of your life. Preparing food should be enjoyable, and you shouldn't have to stress to make meals that are healthy and delicious. But how many times have you felt like you're falling short because there aren't enough hours in the day to prepare all your meals? How many times have you viewed meal preparation as an unpleasant chore?

I worked for decades as a professional chef, but at home I had the same challenges as everyone else. I certainly did not want to spend hours each day in my own kitchen making healthy meals for my family. My husband, who worked early morning shifts and watched our small children while I worked the afternoon shifts, was overwhelmed as well. I remember the tipping point more than 20 years ago like it was yesterday; dinner one evening was crackers and peanut butter because my husband and I were justifiably exhausted. Enough was enough—there had to be a better way.

So I started to plan a weekly cooking day, putting together prep plans designed around limited-ingredient recipes to make things easy. It worked beautifully and freed up valuable time we then spent playing, relaxing, and living. I started a personal chef business to create these convenient weekly packages for clients and—no surprise—had too much work almost immediately. The need for nutritious, satisfying meals is universal, as is the desire to spend precious free time productively; that's where this 12-week meal prep plan comes in.

Since you picked up this book, you must be interested in testing the meal prep waters, and the comprehensive plan found in these pages will help you swim! The next 12 weeks are laid out concisely and clearly with shopping lists, a step-by-step prep plan for your cooking day, and, of course, five delicious five-ingredient recipes per week. Don't worry, these short recipes are long on flavor and texture—you will not be disappointed.

This book will provide all the information you need to successfully and safely prep and store meals that will delight and nourish you week after week. There are also 40 five-ingredient bonus recipes in part 2 to expand your meal prep repertoire even further. Let's get started!

Clockwise from left: Chocolate Cashew Bars, page 19; Honey Sesame Salmon with Squash, page 68; Chicken Cobb Salad, page 26; Roasted Red Pepper Spread, page 109

PART I:

Simplifying MEAL PREP

In this chapter you will learn the basics of meal prep, which will free up valuable time in your life and still allow you to eat healthy, delicious meals every day. The techniques and best practices to maximize your meal prep, as well as the best containers to use for your specific lifestyle, will be laid out clearly. Setting up your kitchen with essential equipment and basic pantry items for the 12-week plan will be a snap. Finally, we'll discuss food safety and how to ensure that your carefully prepared meals will stay fresh all week long.

Honey Sesame Salmon with Squash, page 68

The Fundamentals

The meal prep in this book will cover 12 weeks; everything in the process is outlined right down to the last ingredient and storage container so that you can dive right in. There is a misconception that more ingredients equals more flavor. This is not true, as you will find when you dive into the meal plan recipes in this book. There are few things more intimidating than an ingredient list that is as long as your shopping list, especially if you are a beginner in the kitchen or have a tight schedule. To make your 12-week plan as simple as possible, the ingredients in each dish are kept to a minimum so that you can concentrate on becoming familiar with cooking five days' worth of dishes effectively. If you want to add a favorite herb or topping to a recipe, go right ahead! The following are just a few benefits of limited-ingredient dishes.

SAVE TIME

It makes sense that fewer ingredients means less preparation, but it also saves time in other ways. You will spend less time writing out your shopping list and traversing the grocery store looking for ingredients. You'll also save time prepping ingredients. For example, if four recipes have bell peppers, then you dice them all at once and divide among the dishes. With a little practice, your shopping list might only include staples and fewer than 20 other products.

SAVE MONEY

Fewer items on a shopping list equals spending less money. You can also spend a little of your saved time sourcing out whatever deals are available in local stores to knock a few more pennies off your bill. Remember to shop your pantry and refrigerator first. Check off what you already have on hand before you head to the grocery store.

CUT FOOD WASTE

One of the biggest problems in most kitchens is food waste; people buy too much and end up not using the ingredients before they expire, or they have to buy a large quantity of an ingredient they only need a little of. Five-ingredient meal prep recipes help cut down on waste.

EAT HEALTHIER

The recipes in this book focus on whole foods and clean, fresh flavors. With fewer ingredients, the flavors shine through with no heavy sauces or toppings that add calories and fat.

The 5-Ingredient Pantry

You might look at some recipes and think, "Wait a minute, there are more than five ingredients!" You are correct. The ingredient count does not include the following five foundation ingredients that turn up in most recipes, except for desserts. Be sure to always have these ingredients on hand for successful meal prep week after week. In each recipe's ingredient list the non-pantry ingredients will be listed in **bold**.

SALT

Salt perks up the taste of a recipe, teasing your taste buds, especially when added at the end as a finishing seasoning. This book uses sea salt, but you can use kosher or plain table salt.

PEPPER

Pepper adds a hint of heat and will deepen the flavor of the dish. It is not included in every recipe and should be used sparingly because pepper is a powerful spice.

OIL/COOKING SPRAY

Oil is used in many recipes and can add flavor to the finished dish, so choose a high-quality product to enhance the final result.

GARLIC

Garlic can be an acquired taste, so if it is not one of your favorite ingredients, you can leave it out. Garlic is a staple in many cuisines, such as Italian, French, Spanish, and North African.

ONIONS

Soups, stews, eggs, sauces, and many other recipes use onions for flavor and depth. Sweet onions are used in most of the meals in this book because they have a lovely mellow flavor, but you can use any type of onion you like.

Equipment

Every meal prep journey begins with a well-stocked kitchen. To make each week of meal prep a success, you'll need the right tools and equipment. Just as important as the containers you'll store your prepped meals in, the right equipment will make meal prep a breeze. Don't be overwhelmed by the size of the list; you likely have most of these items in your kitchen already.

- Baking and casserole dishes: an assortment of sizes with lids
- Baking sheet: 18 by 13 inches, with a 1-inch-high lip on the sides
- Blender: powerful enough to crush ice easily
- Box grater
- Can opener
- Colander
- Cookware: saucepans (large, medium, and small), a set of non-stick skillets (large, medium, and small), and a stockpot
- Cutting boards
- Immersion blender
- Instant digital thermometer
- Knives (paring knife and chef's knife) and a knife sharpener
- Measuring cups and spoons: wet and dry measuring cups and measuring spoons from ⅛ teaspoon to a tablespoon
- Muffin pan
- Peeler
- Slow cooker
- Spatulas and spoons
- Spiralizer
- Stainless steel bowls: several sizes that stack inside one another
- Whisk (balloon whisk made of metal)

The Art of Storage

The type of containers you choose for your meals is the key to success, but the variety of materials and sizes can be overwhelming. Don't despair—this section will help you sort out your needs and give you an idea of the minimum number of each container you will need for the meal plans in this book. You will need the following:

- 12 (24-ounce) large containers
- 11 (24-ounce) two-compartment containers
- 3 (24-ounce) three-compartment containers
- 10 (16-ounce) medium containers
- 5 (8-ounce) small containers
- 9 (2-ounce) condiment containers

CONTAINER TYPES

The first step in container shopping is to assess your lifestyle. Do you work from home, or do you need to tote meals to work? If carrying meals out of the house, you might find glass containers a bit heavy and maybe a breakage hazard. Also, leak-proof containers with secure snapping lids will be your best friend. No one enjoys cleaning up a spilled meal inside a purse or work bag. It is your personal preference that matters when selecting containers. Keep this in mind as you read through the options.

PLASTIC

Plastic containers are inexpensive, lightweight, stackable (in most cases), dishwasher-safe (in most cases), microwavable (in most cases), and freezer-proof and come in different sizes and configurations, including handy divided compartments. Containers should be durable and leak-proof with snapping, clear lids so that you can see the contents. The most important aspect of plastic containers is that they do not contain BPA (bisphenol A). BPA is a dangerous chemical that can leak into food when these containers are reheated in the microwave. Look for plastic containers with the "BPA-free" label and a number on the bottom indicating that they are food-safe. The numbers 1, 2, 4, or 5 indicate BPA-free containers, and the numbers 3, 6, or 7 mean they're unsafe.

GLASS

Many meal preppers swear by glass containers because they are considered safer, they do not stain, and they are made of eco-friendly, 100-percent recyclable materials. Containers made from borosilicate glass are an excellent choice if you want to take your meals directly from the freezer to the oven. Glass containers are stackable, microwave-safe, freezer-safe, dishwasher-safe, and leak-proof, depending on the product. The lids should be BPA-free plastic. Some lids are not microwave- or dishwasher-safe, so read the packaging to be sure. The drawbacks of glass containers are that they are more expensive, they are heavier, and they can break or crack.

STAINLESS STEEL

Stainless steel containers are suitable for meals that do not have to be reheated. They are not used to store most meals in the refrigerator or freezer. In most cases, they are used for cold meals or wraps and sandwiches. They come with handy dividers, but most are not completely leak-proof. Stainless steel containers are dishwasher-safe but are not suitable for the microwave or freezer. If you do not have access to a microwave where you are going, stainless steel thermal containers are ideal for keeping preheated soup or stew at a perfect hot temperature.

MASON JARS

Mason jars are versatile; you can get jars of varying sizes with latching or screw-top lids, depending on your preference. The glass jars are dishwasher-safe, freezer-safe, and microwavable. Wide-mouth jars can be the most convenient, especially if you are making salads or overnight oats. Mason jars come in different sizes for dressings, sauces, desserts, and even soups and stews. As with other glass containers, this option is heavier than others and can break.

FOOD STORAGE GUIDELINES

This is the most important section of the book because it concerns food safety. Of course, most foods taste best on the day they are prepared; however, with the right recipe and careful attention to cooling, storing, and reheating, the meals will still be delicious throughout the week. It's important to work efficiently during your cook day so that you can get your prepared food sealed, labeled, and into the refrigerator or freezer as quickly as possible. Meal prep recipes can be stored from three days to one week in the refrigerator, depending on the dish's ingredients. The meal plans in this book cover five days, so some of the containers will be placed in the freezer for consumption at the end of the week. These meals might be perfectly fine in the refrigerator for that time, but why not err on the side of caution? The following are some guidelines for successful and safe meal prep storage.

PREPPING

Successful and safe meals start with good kitchen hygiene. Make sure you frequently wash your hands and equipment throughout the cooking day to avoid cross-contamination. Oversee the steps of your prep carefully, and leave items such as dairy or meat in the refrigerator until just before you need them. Make sure the ingredients used in your recipes are fresh, and check your refrigerator to ensure it is set for 40ºF or lower for safe-food storage.

COOKING

Cook meat and poultry completely to 145ºF and 165ºF, respectively. Slightly undercook your pasta and grains if storing so that they don't become too soft when reheating. Use garlic in your meals whenever appropriate because it is a powerful antibacterial. A squeeze of lemon juice on just-cooked foods can also halt the enzyme action that causes spoilage.

COOLING

Divide the cooked recipes into the containers immediately and refrigerate—food cools faster in small amounts. If you have cooked poultry or meat topping a salad, cool the cooked item completely before adding it to the dish. Bacteria grow between 40ºF and 145ºF, so you want to get your food out of that zone as quickly as possible. Set your containers apart in the refrigerator for increased airflow and quicker cooling.

PROPER LABELING

Every single component of your meal prep meals needs a label on it before it is placed in the refrigerator or freezer or even on the counter at room temperature. This is a crucial step—at a minimum, write the preparation date and name of the dish. You can also put the day by which to eat the dish and reheating instructions, if desired. You can use standard sticker labels, labels designed to dissolve in the dishwasher (leaving no residue), or printable labels.

STORING

Do not overcrowd your containers in the refrigerator, as airflow is important to maintain the correct temperature. Make sure the containers are completely sealed because oxygen can encourage spoilage. If you are freezing your meals, make sure they are completely cooled and in a well-sealed container before freezing. The meals in this book will only be frozen for four or fewer days, so there should be no loss of quality.

THAWING

Thaw your frozen meals in the refrigerator overnight (in general, about 12 hours), and never on the counter. There are other methods, but to ensure quality and safety, stick with this process.

REHEATING

The recipes in this book are designed to be reheated in the microwave, but you can certainly use the stovetop for soups or stews. The essential part of reheating is to bring your food to 165°F. This might take several 30-second intervals, or you can use a reheat setting if your microwave has one. If possible, stir the food in the middle of the process to distribute the heat evenly. Once reheated, the meal must be discarded if you do not finish it.

What to Expect from Meal Preps and Recipes

Welcome to the heart of the book! This is where two culinary concepts designed to streamline your life—meal prep and five-ingredient recipes—combine for the ultimate simplified 12-week prep plan. Each week includes five delectable recipes and a shopping list. Keep in mind the meal plans are designed for one person, so be sure to double the recipes if you're prepping for two. There is also a step-by-step prep schedule to walk you through your cooking day so that your time is used efficiently. Three months' worth of meal prep plans means no stress required, and after the 12 weeks are done, you can either plan your own weeks or start over again.

    The recipes include only ingredients that will be easy to find at your local store. The combination of the five dishes for the week requires about two and a half hours of active time in the kitchen on your cook day (not including slow cooker meals or cooling time). Each recipe also has handy labels indicating whether the meal is dairy-free, gluten-free, nut-free, vegan, or vegetarian.

Refrigerator/Freezer Storage Chart

FOOD	REFRIGERATOR	FREEZER
Poultry (parts)	1–2 days	9 months
Meat (beef, pork, lamb)	3–5 days	4–12 months
Ground meats (beef, pork, chicken, turkey, lamb)	1–2 days	3–4 months
Bacon	1 week	1 month
Sausage (beef, pork, chicken, turkey)	1–2 days	1–2 months
Fish	1–2 days	3–8 months
Fresh shrimp, crab, scallops, squid	1–2 days	3–6 months
Eggs (in the shell)	3–5 weeks	Do not freeze
Hard cheeses (Parmesan)	4 months	6 months
Semi-hard cheeses (cheddar, Swiss, Havarti)	6 months	6 months
Butter	3 months	6 months
Milk	1 week	1 month
Tofu	3 weeks	5 months
Yogurt	2 weeks	2 months
Frozen vegetables	Do not refrigerate	8–12 months
Frozen fruit	Do not refrigerate	8–12 months
Soups and stews	3–5 days	2–4 months
Cooked meats and meat dishes	3–5 days	2–3 months
Cooked fish	3–4 days	4–6 months
Egg quiches, omelets, frittatas	3–5 days	2 months

CHAPTER 1

Week 1 Prep

Western Omelet Sandwiches 15

Crunchy Lettuce Cajun Coleslaw Wraps 16

Spicy Vegetarian Chili 17

Cheesy Chicken Broccoli Casserole 18

Chocolate Cashew Bars 19

Your first week in this meal prep experience will give you a good idea of what to expect for the next three months. We are going to start slowly, with only two proteins and a short shopping list that includes products you might already have on hand, such as rice, canned legumes, spices, and herbs. Be aware that you can substitute simple items such as black beans or lentils for the great northern beans in this menu, or white rice for brown rice. Remember, the aim is to make your meal prep as easy and quick as possible but also fun, so enjoy yourself!

Chocolate Cashew Bars, page 19

SHOPPING LIST

5-INGREDIENT PANTRY

- *Black pepper, freshly ground*
- *Garlic, minced (5 teaspoons)*
- *Oil, olive (1 tablespoon)*
- *Onion, sweet (2)*
- *Salt, sea*

MEAT, POULTRY, SEAFOOD

- Chicken, 2 (4-ounce) boneless, skinless breasts
- Ham, lean, cooked (4 ounces)

DAIRY AND NONDAIRY SUBSTITUTES

- Butter (6 tablespoons), salted
- Eggs, large (8)
- Parmesan cheese, grated (½ cup)

PRODUCE

- Bell peppers, green (3)
- Broccoli (1 head)
- Coleslaw mix (6 cups, or about 20 ounces)
- Lettuce, iceberg (1 head)

CANNED AND JARRED

- Black beans, low-sodium (1 [15-ounce] can)
- Coleslaw dressing (½ cup)
- Great northern beans, low-sodium (1 [15-ounce] can)
- Tomatoes, diced, low-sodium (1 [28-ounce] can)

PANTRY

- Cajun seasoning (1 tablespoon)
- Cashews, roasted, chopped (1 cup)
- Chicken broth, low-sodium (½ cup)
- Chili powder (2 tablespoons)
- Chocolate chips, dark (½ cup)
- Honey (½ cup)
- Oats, rolled (2 cups)
- Rice, brown (¾ cup)

OTHER

- English muffins, whole-wheat (5)
- Soy crumbles (such as Gardein Beefless Ground) (1 [13.7-ounce] bag)

	BREAKFAST	LUNCH	DINNER	SNACK/DESSERT
DAY 1	Western Omelet Sandwich	Crunchy Lettuce Cajun Coleslaw Wraps	Spicy Vegetarian Chili	Chocolate Cashew Bars
DAY 2	Western Omelet Sandwich	Crunchy Lettuce Cajun Coleslaw Wraps	Cheesy Chicken Broccoli Casserole	Chocolate Cashew Bars
DAY 3	Western Omelet Sandwich	Spicy Vegetarian Chili	Cheesy Chicken Broccoli Casserole	Crunchy Lettuce Cajun Coleslaw Wraps
DAY 4	Western Omelet Sandwich	Crunchy Lettuce Cajun Coleslaw Wraps	Spicy Vegetarian Chili	Chocolate Cashew Bars
DAY 5	Western Omelet Sandwich	Spicy Vegetarian Chili	Cheesy Chicken Broccoli Casserole	Chocolate Cashew Bars

STEP-BY-STEP PREP

THE NIGHT BEFORE YOUR COOKING DAY

1. Place ¾ cup of brown rice and 3 cups of water in a medium container, seal it, and soak the rice overnight in the refrigerator.

ON YOUR COOKING DAY

1. Take out all the vegetables required for the week.
   - Chop 3 bell peppers.
   - Chop 2 onions.
   - Cut 1 head of broccoli into small florets.
   - Remove the core from 1 head of iceberg lettuce and separate 12 roughly equal-size leaves.

2. Prepare the Spicy Vegetarian Chili (page 17) using 2 cups of chopped green pepper and 1 cup of chopped onion. Place all the ingredients in the slow cooker and start it.

3. Prepare the Crunchy Lettuce Cajun Coleslaw Wraps (page 16) completely. Stack three lettuce leaves in 1 compartment each of 4 large (2-compartment) containers. Evenly divide the filling into the other side of the containers, about 2 cups for each meal. Seal the containers, label, and store in the refrigerator.

4. To make the Western Omelet Sandwiches (page 15), chop the ham and whisk the eggs. Prepare the egg part of the sandwiches completely, using the remaining chopped green pepper and ½ cup of chopped onion. Cool the eggs as directed.

5. Preheat the oven to 350°F and prepare the baking dish for the Chocolate Cashew Bars (page 19).

6. Prepare the bars completely, setting them aside to cool in the refrigerator. Leave the oven on.

7. When the bars are put in the refrigerator, take out the cooled eggs and assemble the sandwiches. Place each sandwich in a small plastic bag, squeeze out the air, and seal. Label the sandwiches and store 3 of them in the refrigerator and 2 in the freezer.

8. Cut the chicken for the Cheesy Chicken Broccoli Casserole (page 18).

9. Prepare the casserole as directed, bake, and divide the casserole evenly among 3 large containers and place them in the refrigerator to cool completely, about 1 hour.

10. When firm enough to cut, take the Chocolate Cashew Bars out of the refrigerator and slice into 9 bars. Place 4 bars into sealable plastic bags, label, and store in the refrigerator for up to 1 week. Place the other 5 bars in a larger bag, seal, label, and store in the freezer for up to 1 month.

11. When the Cheesy Chicken Casserole is cooled, seal, label, and store 2 containers in the refrigerator for up to 3 days and 1 in the freezer for up to 2 months.

12. Evenly divide the chili among 4 large meal prep containers and set in the refrigerator to cool.

13. When the chili is cooled, seal, label, and store 2 containers in the refrigerator for up to 4 days and 2 in the freezer for up to 1 month.

NUT-FREE

WESTERN OMELET SANDWICHES

SERVINGS: 5 • **PREP TIME:** 15 minutes • **COOK TIME:** 12 minutes

Fluffy eggs, savory ham, slightly crunchy green pepper, and flavorful onion come together perfectly as a filling sandwich on an English muffin. You can also create easy wraps with this filling or accessorize the meal with a slice of cheese and a splash of hot sauce.

2 tablespoons butter

1 green bell pepper, seeded and chopped

½ sweet onion, chopped

½ cup finely chopped lean ham

8 large eggs

5 whole-wheat English muffins

Sea salt

Freshly ground black pepper

1. In a large skillet over medium-high heat, melt the butter.
2. Sauté the bell pepper, onion, and ham until softened, 5 to 6 minutes.
3. In a medium bowl, whisk the eggs, then pour them into the skillet, tilting to combine with the other ingredients. Cook until the eggs are just cooked through and set, about 6 minutes.
4. Remove the skillet from the heat and cut the cooked eggs into 5 roughly equal portions. Transfer the eggs to a plate and set aside in the refrigerator to cool completely.
5. When the eggs are cool, divide them evenly among the English muffins and lightly season each with salt and black pepper.

REHEATING TIP: Reheat by wrapping the sandwich in a paper towel and microwaving for 30-second intervals until heated through.

SUBSTITUTION TIP: Bacon, sausage, or chopped chicken instead of ham is delicious in these simple sandwiches.

Per serving: Calories: 341; Total Fat: 16g; Saturated Fat: 6g; Protein: 20g; Total Carbs: 32g; Fiber: 5g; Sugar: 8g; Sodium: 543mg

GLUTEN-FREE • NUT-FREE • VEGETARIAN

CRUNCHY LETTUCE CAJUN COLESLAW WRAPS

SERVINGS: 4 • **PREP TIME:** 10 minutes

Lettuce wraps are not a new culinary invention; this dish has been around in different forms for thousands of years in Asia and is enjoyed globally today. If you are not allergic to nuts, top your wraps with a generous scattering of chopped roasted cashews for a satisfying crunchy texture.

6 cups coleslaw mix

½ cup store-bought creamy coleslaw dressing

4 cups soy crumbles, thawed

1 tablespoon Cajun seasoning

1 head iceberg lettuce, cored and 12 equal-size leaves separated

1. In a large bowl, toss together the coleslaw mix and the dressing until well combined.
2. In a medium bowl, stir together the soy crumbles and Cajun seasoning and add them to the coleslaw mixture, tossing to mix thoroughly.
3. When ready to eat, scoop the filling into the lettuce leaves, fold them up, and enjoy!

SUBSTITUTION TIP: Try taco seasoning, Middle Eastern seasoning, or your favorite spices and herbs to create unique combinations. The coleslaw is mild enough to combine beautifully with any seasoning.

Per serving: Calories: 307; Total Fat: 10g; Saturated Fat: 1g; Protein: 26g; Total Carbs: 32g; Fiber: 9g; Sugar: 19g; Sodium: 960mg

DAIRY-FREE • GLUTEN-FREE • NUT-FREE • VEGAN

SPICY VEGETARIAN CHILI

SERVINGS: 4 • **PREP TIME:** 10 minutes • **COOK TIME:** 2 to 3 hours

Chili is perfect for meal prep menus because it gets more flavorful the longer it sits in the refrigerator, and freezes beautifully. This vegetarian version can be bulked up with a couple of cups of soy crumbles if you want to mimic ground beef. Try using chipotle chili powder for a rich, smoky flavor or habanero chili powder to add some real heat.

Nonstick cooking spray

1 (28-ounce) can low-sodium diced tomatoes, with their juices

1 (15-ounce) can low-sodium black beans, with liquid

1 (15-ounce) can low-sodium great northern beans, with liquid

2 green bell peppers, seeded and chopped

1 sweet onion, chopped

1 tablespoon minced garlic

2 tablespoons chili powder

1. Lightly oil the insert of a slow cooker with the cooking spray.
2. Place the tomatoes, black beans, great northern beans, peppers, onion, garlic, and chili powder in the slow cooker and stir.
3. Cover and cook on high for 2 to 3 hours or until the vegetables are tender and the chili is thick.

REHEATING TIP: To reheat, microwave uncovered for 30-second intervals until heated through. If reheating from frozen, thaw the chili in the refrigerator overnight before reheating as directed.

SERVING TIP: Serve with sour cream and shredded cheddar. You can also use tortilla chips to scoop up the chili.

Per serving: Calories: 293; Total Fat: 2g; Saturated Fat: 0g; Protein: 16g; Total Carbs: 56g; Fiber: 16g; Sugar: 16g; Sodium: 470mg

GLUTEN-FREE • NUT-FREE

CHEESY CHICKEN BROCCOLI CASSEROLE

SERVINGS: 3 • **PREP TIME:** 15 minutes • **COOK TIME:** 50 to 55 minutes

If you lived through the '90s, the recipe Chicken Divine should ring a bell. This is an incredibly simplified version of that dish, sans the sodium-packed cream of chicken soup base and handfuls of cheese. You can add more Parmesan cheese if you wish, or you can top the casserole with buttered bread crumbs to mimic the original more closely.

1 head broccoli, cut into small florets

¾ cup brown rice, soaked overnight in 3 cups water

1½ cups water

1 tablespoon olive oil, divided

2 (4-ounce) boneless, skinless chicken breasts, cut into 1-inch cubes

½ sweet onion, chopped

2 teaspoons minced garlic

½ cup grated Parmesan cheese

½ cup low-sodium chicken broth

Sea salt

Freshly ground black pepper

1. Preheat the oven to 350°F.
2. Place a large saucepan filled with water over high heat and bring to a boil. Blanch the broccoli for 1 minute, drain, and rinse in cold water. Set aside.
3. Drain the rice and combine with the 1½ cups of water in a large saucepan over high heat. Bring to a boil, cover, reduce the heat to low, and simmer until the liquid is absorbed, 20 to 25 minutes.
4. While the rice is cooking, heat the oil in a medium non-stick oven-proof skillet over medium-high heat. Sauté the chicken until it is just cooked through, about 10 minutes. Add the onion and garlic and sauté until softened, about 3 minutes. Remove from heat.
5. When the rice is cooked, stir it into the chicken mixture with the broccoli, cheese, and broth.
6. Season lightly with salt and pepper, cover with foil, and bake for 30 minutes, until heated through and the cheese is melted.

REHEATING TIP: To reheat, microwave for 30-second intervals until heated through. If reheating from frozen, thaw in the refrigerator overnight before reheating as directed.

Per serving: Calories: 461; Total Fat: 13g; Saturated Fat: 5g; Protein: 32g; Total Carbs: 56g; Fiber: 7g; Sugar: 7g; Sodium: 387mg

GLUTEN-FREE • VEGETARIAN

CHOCOLATE CASHEW BARS

MAKES: 9 bars • **PREP TIME:** 5 minutes • **COOK TIME:** 10 minutes

For many people, chocolate is its own food group. These bars taste like a cross between a granola bar and a chocolate bar—decadent and healthy at the same time. You can change up the nuts to create different flavor combinations; try peanuts or hazelnuts.

2 cups rolled oats

1 cup roasted cashews, roughly chopped

½ cup honey

4 tablespoons butter

½ cup dark chocolate chips

1. Preheat the oven to 350°F degrees. Line a 9-inch square baking dish and a baking sheet with parchment paper.

2. Spread the oats and nuts on the baking sheet and toast lightly until golden, about 10 minutes, then transfer to a large bowl.

3. While the oats are toasting, stir together the honey and butter in a small saucepan over medium heat. Heat until the butter is melted and the mixture is smooth and bubbly, about 4 minutes.

4. Remove the butter mixture from the heat. Pour over the oat mixture and stir until very well mixed. Let cool for 15 minutes.

5. Add the chocolate chips, stir to combine, and firmly press the oat mixture into the baking dish. Chill the bars in the refrigerator until completely cooled, about 1 hour.

6. Lift the bars out of the baking dish using the parchment paper and cut them into 9 (3-inch) square bars.

INGREDIENT TIP: Cashews are an excellent source of magnesium, copper, and oleic acid. These delicious nuts can help stabilize blood sugar, lower bad cholesterol, and reduce the risk of heart disease and cancer.

Per serving: Calories: 361; Total Fat: 17g; Saturated Fat: 6g; Protein: 9g; Total Carbs: 47g; Fiber: 5g; Sugar: 19g; Sodium: 45mg

CHAPTER 2

Week 2 Prep

Apple Pie Overnight Oats 25

Chicken Cobb Salad 26

Spaghetti Bolognese 27

Salmon, Potato, and French Bean Sheet-Pan Bake 28

Spicy Snack Mix 29

Week two of meal prep uses simple overnight oats, a beloved pasta dish, and the first quick sheet-pan dinner, so your prep and cooking times for all five recipes should be about two and a half hours without rushing (not including cooling time). The trick to week two is overlapping the cooking and prep times because you will be using different appliances for everything. You can pick up a kitchen timer that can set six to eight times at once and program your cook times as you go.

Chicken Cobb Salad, page 26

SHOPPING LIST

5-INGREDIENT PANTRY

- *Black pepper, freshly ground*
- *Garlic, minced (4 teaspoons)*
- *Oil, olive (5 tablespoons)*
- *Onion, sweet (1)*
- *Salt, sea*

MEAT, POULTRY, OR SEAFOOD

- Beef, ground, extra-lean (1 pound)
- Chicken, 3 (4-ounce) boneless, skinless breasts
- Salmon, 3 (5-ounce) fillets

DAIRY

- Blue cheese (3 ounces)
- Milk, 2 percent (1½ cups)
- Parmesan cheese, grated (½ cup)
- Yogurt, Greek, vanilla (1 cup)

PRODUCE

- Apples (2)
- French beans (1 pound)
- Lettuce, romaine (1 head)
- Potatoes, russet, medium (3)
- Tomatoes, large (3)

CANNED AND JARRED

- Balsamic dressing (6 tablespoons)
- Maple syrup (5 tablespoons)
- Tomatoes, crushed, low-sodium (3 [15-ounce] cans)

PANTRY

- Almonds, whole, raw (1 cup)
- Basil, dried (1 tablespoon)
- Cayenne powder (¼ teaspoon)
- Cheerios (1 cup)
- Lemon pepper seasoning (1 tablespoon)
- Oats, rolled (1½ cups)
- Pecans, whole, raw (1 cup)
- Pretzel sticks, small (1 cup)
- Spaghetti, dry (8 ounces)

	BREAKFAST	LUNCH	DINNER	SNACK/DESSERT
DAY 1	Apple Pie Overnight Oats	Chicken Cobb Salad	Salmon, Potato, and French Bean Sheet-Pan Bake	Spicy Snack Mix
DAY 2	Apple Pie Overnight Oats	Salmon, Potato, and French Bean Sheet-Pan Bake	Spaghetti Bolognese	Spicy Snack Mix
DAY 3	Apple Pie Overnight Oats	Spaghetti Bolognese	Salmon, Potato, and French Bean Sheet-Pan Bake	Spicy Snack Mix
DAY 4	Apple Pie Overnight Oats	Chicken Cobb Salad	Spaghetti Bolognese	Spicy Snack Mix
DAY 5	Apple Pie Overnight Oats	Chicken Cobb Salad	Spaghetti Bolognese	Spicy Snack Mix

STEP-BY-STEP PREP

1. Preheat the oven to 350°F.
2. Make the Spicy Snack Mix (page 29) and place in the oven.
3. While the snack mix is roasting, make the Apple Pie Overnight Oats (page 25). Place in 5 medium containers and seal, label, and refrigerate for up to 5 days.
4. Cut the chicken for the Chicken Cobb Salad (page 26), sauté it, and set aside in the refrigerator to cool.
5. Cut the potatoes and trim the beans for the Salmon, Potato, and French Bean Sheet-Pan Bake (page 28) and prepare as directed, placing the baking sheet in the oven.

6. Prepare the sauce for the Spaghetti Bolognese (page 27), and while it is cooking, make the spaghetti and remove the salmon and vegetables from the oven at the 15- to 18-minute mark.

7. Evenly divide the salmon, potatoes, and green beans among 3 large (3-compartment) containers and store in the refrigerator for up to 3 days.

8. Evenly divide the spaghetti among 4 large containers and top with the sauce. Sprinkle each with 2 tablespoons of Parmesan cheese. Seal, label, and store 2 of the containers in the refrigerator for up to 3 days and 2 in the freezer for up to 1 month.

9. Take the cooled chicken out of the refrigerator and prepare the salad. Divide the dressing among 3 large meal prep containers. Divide the chicken, blue cheese, and tomatoes into each container. Add 2 cups of romaine to each container, seal, label, and store in the refrigerator for up to 5 days.

10. Transfer the cooled Spicy Snack Mix to 5 small sealable bags, about ¾ cup each. Store the snack mix at room temperature for up to 1 week.

GLUTEN-FREE • NUT-FREE • VEGETARIAN

APPLE PIE OVERNIGHT OATS

SERVINGS: 5 • **PREP TIME:** 15 minutes

Overnight oats is one of the easiest breakfasts to throw together even when you aren't meal planning. Simply stir all the ingredients together in a bowl or jar and put it in the refrigerator. Oats do not contain gluten naturally but may be manufactured in plants that handle other gluten-containing products, so check your label if this is a concern. Overnight oats can get a little soggy the longer they sit in the refrigerator, so heat up your last portion to improve the texture.

- 1½ **cups rolled oats**
- 1½ **cups 2 percent milk**
- 1 **cup vanilla Greek yogurt**
- 5 **tablespoons maple syrup**
- 2 **small apples, cored, peeled, and chopped**

Divide the oats, milk, yogurt, maple syrup, and apples among 5 medium meal prep containers. Stir until very well combined and refrigerate overnight.

> **SERVING TIP:** This breakfast can be enjoyed cold or warm. To serve warm, take off the lid and microwave the oats for 45 to 60 seconds, adding extra milk if the texture is too thick.

Per serving: Calories: 332; Total Fat: 6g; Saturated Fat: 2g; Protein: 12g; Total Carbs: 58g; Fiber: 6g; Sugar: 24g; Sodium: 61mg

GLUTEN-FREE • NUT-FREE

CHICKEN COBB SALAD

SERVINGS: 3 • **PREP TIME:** 15 minutes • **COOK TIME:** 15 minutes

Cobb salad was a signature dish in the 1930s at the Brown Derby restaurant in Hollywood. This is not a traditional version of the salad, but rather an adapted recipe that works better for meal prep. The original includes four types of lettuce, bacon, hard-boiled eggs, and avocado in addition to the ingredients found in this salad. You can certainly add these extras when preparing your salads, but make sure you add the avocado right before serving.

3 (4-ounce) boneless, skinless chicken breasts, diced

Sea salt

1 tablespoon olive oil

6 tablespoons store-bought balsamic dressing or Simple Herbed Balsamic Dressing (page 174)

3 ounces crumbled blue cheese

3 large tomatoes, diced

6 cups chopped romaine lettuce

1. Season the chicken with salt.
2. In a large skillet over medium-high heat, heat the oil and sauté the chicken until cooked through, about 15 minutes.
3. Remove the chicken from the skillet to a plate, and cool completely in the refrigerator.
4. Assemble the salad by combining the dressing, chicken, blue cheese, tomatoes, and lettuce.

SERVING TIP: You can layer the salads into wide-mouth mason jars if you like that presentation style. Just put the ingredients in the jars in the same order as directed in step 4.

Per serving: Calories: 353; Total Fat: 16g; Saturated Fat: 6g; Protein: 35g; Total Carbs: 16g; Fiber: 4g; Sugar: 10g; Sodium: 365mg

NUT-FREE

SPAGHETTI BOLOGNESE

SERVINGS: 4 • **PREP TIME:** 10 minutes • **COOK TIME:** 40 minutes

Anyone who has made a huge pot of pasta and sauce knows this type of meal seems to last forever in the refrigerator with no loss of quality or taste. It even freezes well! If you enjoy a spicier sauce, add a pinch or two of red pepper flakes along with the basil.

1 tablespoon olive oil

1 pound extra-lean ground beef

1 sweet onion, chopped

1 tablespoon minced garlic

3 (15-ounce) cans sodium-free crushed tomatoes

1 tablespoon dried basil

8 ounces dry spaghetti

Sea salt

Freshly ground black pepper

½ cup grated Parmesan cheese

1. In a large skillet or saucepan over medium-high heat, heat the oil and sauté the ground beef until it is cooked through and browned, about 7 minutes. Add the onion and garlic and sauté until the vegetables are softened, about 3 minutes.

2. Add the tomatoes and basil and bring to a boil, then reduce the heat to low and simmer for about 30. Remove from heat and season with salt and pepper.

3. While the sauce is simmering, bring a large saucepan of water to a boil and cook the pasta according to the package instructions until al dente. Drain the pasta and transfer back to the saucepan.

4. Add about ½ cup of the Bolognese sauce to the pasta, tossing to coat, so the pasta does not stick together. Garnish with Parmesan cheese.

REHEATING TIP: To reheat, microwave for 30-second intervals until heated through. If reheating from frozen, thaw in the refrigerator overnight before reheating as directed.

Per serving: Calories: 526; Total Fat: 14g; Saturated Fat: 5g; Protein: 39g; Total Carbs: 63g; Fiber: 9g; Sugar: 14g; Sodium: 345mg

DAIRY-FREE • GLUTEN-FREE • NUT-FREE

SALMON, POTATO, and FRENCH BEAN SHEET-PAN BAKE

SERVINGS: 3 • **PREP TIME:** 15 minutes • **COOK TIME:** 30 to 33 minutes

Sheet-pan dinners are a staple for meal prep because an entire recipe can be made quickly with little effort. You can do other tasks while the protein, starch, and vegetables roast to perfection in the oven. Salmon is a nice fish for roasting because it is packed with natural oils that keep it moist and flavorful, even if you overcook it a smidge.

3 medium russet potatoes, cut into eighths

2 tablespoons olive oil, divided

1 teaspoon minced garlic

3 (5-ounce) salmon fillets

1 tablespoon lemon pepper seasoning

1 pound French beans

Sea salt

Freshly ground black pepper

1. Preheat the oven to 400°F. Line a baking sheet with parchment paper.
2. In a large bowl, toss the potatoes with 1½ tablespoons of oil and the garlic until well coated. Arrange them on one-half of the baking sheet and bake for 15 minutes.
3. While the potatoes are roasting, rub the salmon with the lemon pepper seasoning. In a medium bowl, toss the French beans with the remaining ½ tablespoon of oil and season them with salt and pepper.
4. After 15 minutes, remove the potatoes from the oven and arrange the salmon fillets on one remaining quarter of the baking sheet and the green beans on the other quarter.
5. Flip the potatoes, then place the baking sheet back in the oven and roast until the salmon flakes when pressed with a fork and the potatoes and green beans are tender, 15 to 18 minutes.

REHEATING TIP: To reheat, microwave for 30-second intervals until heated through.

Per serving: Calories: 613; Total Fat: 18g; Saturated Fat: 8g; Protein: 40g; Total Carbs: 73g; Fiber: 8g; Sugar: 3g; Sodium: 94mg

DAIRY-FREE • VEGAN

SPICY SNACK MIX

MAKES: 4 cups • **PREP TIME:** 10 minutes • **COOK TIME:** 15 minutes

Snack mixes are versatile, made from almost any combination of candies—nuts, dried fruit, cereal, crackers, pretzels, or corn nuts. The mixture can change depending on your palate or specific dietary needs. This version contains heart-friendly nuts and high-fiber cereal, which will help keep you full and satiated.

1 cup whole raw almonds

1 cup whole raw pecans

1 tablespoon olive oil

¼ teaspoon cayenne powder

1 cup Cheerios

1 cup small pretzel sticks

Sea salt

1. Preheat the oven to 350°F and line a baking sheet with parchment paper.

2. In a large bowl, toss together the almonds, pecans, oil, and cayenne until well coated.

3. Spread the nut mixture on the baking sheet and bake until lightly toasted, stirring once, about 15 minutes.

4. Transfer the roasted nuts back to the large bowl and add the Cheerios and pretzels. Season with salt and set aside to cool, about 2 hours. Give the mix an occasional stir while it cools so that it doesn't clump together.

SUBSTITUTION TIP: The ingredients in this savory mixture can be changed depending on your palate. Try different nuts, cereals, or little cheese crackers to create unique combinations.

Per serving: Calories: 377; Total Fat: 31g; Saturated Fat: 3g; Protein: 9g; Total Carbs: 20g; Fiber: 7g; Sugar: 2g; Sodium: 64mg

CHAPTER 3

Week 3 Prep

Fluffy Buttermilk Pancakes 35

Sesame Zoodles with Summer Vegetables 36

Shawarma Chicken with Root Vegetables 37

Marinated Flank Steak with Pico de Gallo 38

Lemon Mascarpone Cream Sauce with Strawberries 39

Week three is decadent, designed to show you that simple five-ingredient recipes can be exciting and delicious. Buttermilk pancakes, globally inspired salad and chicken meals, tender steak, and a creamy fruit snack should keep you looking forward to your meals all week long. Two meals prepared on sheet pans and a quick dip cut down on prep time so that you will not be tied to the kitchen all day. Remember to check your pantry, refrigerator, and freezer for existing supplies before heading out to get your groceries.

Shawarma Chicken with Root Vegetables, page 37

SHOPPING LIST

5-INGREDIENT PANTRY

- *Garlic, minced (2 teaspoons)*
- *Oil, olive (3 tablespoons)*
- *Oil, vegetable (2 tablespoons)*
- *Onion, sweet (1)*
- *Salt, sea*

MEAT, POULTRY, OR SEAFOOD

- Chicken, 4 (4-ounce) boneless, skinless breasts
- Steak, flank (1 pound)

DAIRY AND NONDAIRY SUBSTITUTES

- Buttermilk (1½ cups)
- Eggs, large (1)
- Mascarpone cheese (¾ cup)
- Yogurt, Greek, vanilla (½ cup)

PRODUCE

- Berries (2½ cups)
- Carrots (2)
- Celeriac (1)
- Lemon (1)
- Parsnips (4)
- Strawberries (2½ pounds)
- Sweet potatoes (2)
- Zucchini (3)

CANNED AND JARRED

- Sesame dressing (such as Kraft Asian Sesame or Bragg Ginger and Sesame) (6 tablespoons)
- Balsamic vinaigrette (½ cup)
- Honey (2 tablespoons)
- Maple syrup (10 ounces)
- Salsa (¾ cup)

PANTRY

- Baking powder (1 tablespoon)
- Chicken broth, low-sodium (1½ cups)
- Flour, all-purpose (1¾ cups)
- Rice, basmati (¾ cup)
- Sesame seeds (¼ cup)
- Shawarma spice (2 tablespoons)
- Spaghetti, whole-wheat, dry (6 ounces)
- Sugar (2 tablespoons)

	BREAKFAST	LUNCH	DINNER	SNACK/DESSERT
DAY 1	Fluffy Buttermilk Pancakes	Sesame Zoodles with Summer Vegetables	Shawarma Chicken with Root Vegetables	Lemon Mascarpone Cream Sauce with Strawberries
DAY 2	Fluffy Buttermilk Pancakes	Sesame Zoodles with Summer Vegetables	Marinated Flank Steak with Pico de Gallo	Lemon Mascarpone Cream Sauce with Strawberries
DAY 3	Fluffy Buttermilk Pancakes	Sesame Zoodles with Summer Vegetables	Shawarma Chicken with Root Vegetables	Lemon Mascarpone Cream Sauce with Strawberries
DAY 4	Fluffy Buttermilk Pancakes	Shawarma Chicken with Root Vegetables	Marinated Flank Steak with Pico de Gallo	Lemon Mascarpone Cream Sauce with Strawberries
DAY 5	Fluffy Buttermilk Pancakes	Marinated Flank Steak with Pico de Gallo	Shawarma Chicken with Root Vegetables	Lemon Mascarpone Cream Sauce with Strawberries

STEP-BY-STEP PREP

1. Marinate the steak for the Marinated Flank Steak with Pico de Gallo (page 38).

2. Prepare the Lemon Mascarpone Cream Sauce with Strawberries (page 39) recipe completely and divide the sauce evenly among 5 large (2-compartment) storage containers, placing it in the smaller section. Place 1 cup of strawberries in the large section of each of the storage containers. Store in the refrigerator for up to 5 days.

3. Prepare the Fluffy Buttermilk Pancakes (page 35) recipe completely and place 2 cooled pancakes in each of 5 medium containers. Pour maple syrup or honey into 5 (2-ounce) containers and seal them. Place berries in 5 small containers. Label all the containers and store them in the refrigerator for up to 5 days.

4. Cook the noodles for the Sesame Zoodles with Summer Vegetables (page 36).

5. While the noodles are cooking, prepare the vegetables for the remaining recipes. For the Shawarma Chicken with Root Vegetables (page 37), peel the parsnips and cut into 1-inch chunks, peel the sweet potatoes and cut into 1-inch chunks, and peel the celeriac and cut into 1-inch pieces. Spiralize the zucchini and carrots for the sesame noodle salad.

6. Cook the rice for the flank steak recipe.

7. Preheat the oven to broil.

8. Remove the steak from the marinade and prepare the meat portion of the recipe. Set the oven to bake at 400°F.

9. Prepare the Sesame Zoodles with Summer Vegetables recipe completely and portion into 3 large meal prep containers, seal, label, and store in the refrigerator for up to 3 days.

10. Season the chicken and prepare the Shawarma Chicken with Root Vegetables recipe completely.

11. Portion the flank steak recipe by transferring the rice to the larger compartment of 3 large (2-compartment) meal prep containers. Slice the steak thinly against the grain, and evenly divide the pieces among the smaller part of each container. Seal, label, and place 1 container in the refrigerator for up to 3 days and 2 in the freezer for up to 1 month. Divide the pico de gallo among 3 small containers, seal, label, and refrigerate for up to 3 days.

12. Divide the vegetables for the shawarma chicken among 4 large (2-compartment) meal prep containers (place in the large side) and place a chicken breast in the smaller side of the container. Seal, label, and place 2 of the containers in the refrigerator for up to 3 days and 2 in the freezer for up to 1 month.

NUT-FREE • VEGETARIAN

FLUFFY BUTTERMILK PANCAKES

SERVINGS: 5 • **PREP TIME:** 10 minutes • **COOK TIME:** 12 minutes

Yes, you can make pancakes in your meal prep menus! This dish keeps very well and freezes beautifully. The toppings suggested here enhance the fluffy golden pancakes, but you can just eat the pancakes plain or with a thin layer of peanut butter. This batter can also be spooned into a waffle maker to create a crunchy variation.

1¾ cups all-purpose flour

2 tablespoons sugar

1 tablespoon baking powder

½ teaspoon sea salt

1½ cups buttermilk

1 large egg

2 tablespoons vegetable oil, plus extra for greasing the skillet

10 ounces maple syrup or honey (optional)

2½ cups berries (optional)

1. In a large bowl, sift together the flour, sugar, baking powder, and salt. Whisk in the buttermilk, egg, and oil until the batter is combined.

2. Heat a large skillet over medium-high heat and lightly grease it with oil.

3. Scoop about ¼ cup of batter per pancake into the skillet and cook until the bubbles on the surface burst, about 2 minutes.

4. Flip the pancakes and cook for 1 to 2 minutes longer until browned on both sides.

5. Repeat with the remaining batter until you have 10 pancakes.

6. Cool the pancakes completely before storing. Serve with maple syrup and/or berries (if using).

SERVING TIP: Eat the pancakes warm or cold. If reheating, wrap the pancakes in a paper towel and microwave for 30 seconds..

INGREDIENT TIP: Do not wash the berries until just before you eat this meal so that they stay fresh.

Per serving: Calories: 449; Total fat: 7g; Saturated fat: 4g; Protein: 9g; Total carbs: 87g; Fiber: 3g; Sugar: 47g; Sodium: 398mg

DAIRY-FREE • NUT-FREE • VEGAN

SESAME ZOODLES *with* SUMMER VEGETABLES

SERVINGS: 3 • **PREP TIME:** 20 minutes • **COOK TIME:** 20 minutes

Spiralized noodles pair fabulously with an assortment of ingredients. They are often used as the only "noodle" in a dish, especially for people looking to cut carbs. This recipe includes whole-wheat spaghetti, which adds a hefty amount of heart-smart fiber to the dish as well.

6 ounces dry whole-wheat spaghetti, broken in half

3 zucchini, spiralized or cut into ribbons with a peeler

2 carrots, spiralized or shredded

6 tablespoons store-bought Asian sesame dressing or Hoisin Dressing and Marinade (page 175)

¼ cup sesame seeds

1. In a medium saucepan over high heat, bring water to a boil. Cook the spaghetti according to the package directions until al dente, about 20 minutes. Drain and rinse in cool water.

2. Place the cooked pasta in a large bowl, add the zucchini, carrots, dressing, and sesame seeds, and toss to combine.

INGREDIENT TIP: To save prep time, you can pick up spiralized zucchini and carrots in the produce section of the supermarket. Check the expiration date and make sure the vegetables will stay fresh for the whole week that you plan to make this dish.

Per serving: Calories: 459; Total fat: 23g; Saturated fat: 3g; Protein: 15g; Total carbs: 57g; Fiber: 9g; Sugar: 9g; Sodium: 354mg

DAIRY-FREE • GLUTEN-FREE • NUT-FREE

SHAWARMA CHICKEN with ROOT VEGETABLES

SERVINGS: 4 • **PREP TIME:** 15 minutes • **COOK TIME:** 40 minutes

Shawarma is a very popular Middle Eastern spice blend used to enhance proteins such as lamb and chicken from street food stalls all the way to Michelin-starred restaurants. The blend is slightly hot and has a pleasing hint of sweetness from the cinnamon. You can either make a batch using the Shawarma Spice Blend recipe or pick up a blend in the grocery store.

4 (4-ounce) boneless, skinless chicken breasts

2 tablespoons store-bought shawarma spice or homemade Shawarma Spice Blend (page 172)

2 tablespoons olive oil, divided

4 parsnips, cut into 1-inch chunks

2 sweet potatoes, cut into 1-inch chunks

1 celeriac, peeled and diced into 1-inch pieces

Sea salt

1. Preheat the oven to 400°F. Line a baking sheet with parchment paper.
2. Rub the chicken breasts all over with the shawarma spice and place them on one-quarter of the baking sheet.
3. In a large bowl, toss together the oil, parsnips, sweet potatoes, and celeriac until the vegetables are well coated. Season the vegetables lightly with salt.
4. Spread the vegetables on the other three-quarters of the baking sheet. Place in the oven and bake until the chicken is cooked through and the vegetables are tender, about 40 minutes, turning the vegetables once halfway through.

REHEATING TIP: To reheat, microwave uncovered for 30-second intervals until heated through. To reheat from frozen, thaw in the refrigerator overnight before reheating as directed.

Per serving: Calories: 390; Total fat: 11g; Saturated fat: 6g; Protein: 29g; Total carbs: 46g; Fiber: 11g; Sugar: 10g; Sodium: 172mg

DAIRY-FREE • GLUTEN-FREE • NUT-FREE

MARINATED FLANK STEAK with PICO DE GALLO

SERVINGS: 3 • **PREP TIME:** 10 minutes, plus marinating time • **COOK TIME:** 37 minutes

Flank steak, or London broil, is an incredibly flavorful cut of beef that is also one of the toughest, so you have to be careful when cooking it. This recipe cooks the steak quickly at high heat to a perfect medium-rare, which is the best temperature for this cut or else it can get rubbery. Slicing it against the grain very thinly to cut through the tough connective tissue ensures a tender texture.

1 pound flank steak

½ cup store-bought balsamic dressing or Simple Herbed Balsamic Dressing (page 174)

1 tablespoon olive oil

1 small sweet onion, chopped

2 teaspoons minced garlic

¾ cup basmati rice

1½ cups low-sodium chicken broth

Sea salt

¾ cup store-bought salsa or Pico de Gallo (page 179)

1. In a resealable bag, marinate the steak with the balsamic dressing and refrigerate for 30 minutes, turning the bag over halfway through.

2. In a large saucepan over medium-high heat, heat the olive oil and sauté the onion and garlic until softened, about 3 minutes.

3. Add the rice and sauté for 2 minutes more. Add the chicken broth and bring the mixture to a boil. Reduce the heat to low, cover, and simmer until the liquid is absorbed and the rice is tender, about 20 minutes. Remove from heat, season with salt, and set aside.

4. While the rice is cooking, preheat the oven to broil.

5. Remove the steak from the marinade, place it on the baking sheet, and let sit at room temperature for 15 minutes. Broil the steak, turning once halfway through, until the meat is medium-rare, 10 to 12 minutes.

6. Remove the steak from the oven and set aside to cool for at least 15 minutes before slicing it against the grain. Serve with the rice and salsa.

REHEATING TIP: To reheat, microwave the rice and steak mixture uncovered in 30-second intervals until just heated through. If frozen, thaw in the refrigerator overnight beforehand.

Per serving: Calories: 522; Total fat: 15g; Saturated fat: 7g; Protein: 40g; Total carbs: 54g; Fiber: 3g; Sugar: 9g; Sodium: 541mg

GLUTEN-FREE • NUT-FREE • VEGETARIAN

LEMON MASCARPONE CREAM SAUCE with STRAWBERRIES

SERVINGS: 5 • **PREP TIME:** 10 minutes

Mascarpone is a double- or triple-cream cheese from Italy with a silky texture and sweet taste. The luscious texture is due to a very high fat content, about 75 percent, roughly twice as much as the more familiar cream cheese. You can substitute cream cheese or crème fraîche for the mascarpone if this delightful, slightly expensive ingredient is not available in your area.

- ¾ cup mascarpone cheese
- ½ cup vanilla Greek yogurt
- Juice and zest of 1 lemon
- 2 tablespoons honey
- 5 cups halved strawberries

In a small bowl, stir together the cheese, yogurt, lemon juice, lemon zest, and honey until well blended. Divide into 5 portions and serve with the strawberries for dipping.

INGREDIENT TIP: Do not wash the berries until you plan to eat each portion. Rinse them under cool water and pat dry with paper towels.

Per serving: Calories: 143; Total fat: 6g; Saturated fat: 3g; Protein: 5g; Total carbs: 20g; Fiber: 3g; Sugar: 16g; Sodium: 151mg

CHAPTER 4

Week 4 Prep

Bacon Breakfast Cassoulet 45

Black Bean Chili Quesadillas 46

Slow Cooker Tomato and Beef Stew 47

Spice-Rubbed Pork Tenderloin 48

Mediterranean Layered Dip 49

You will be multitasking this week, using a slow cooker, a skillet, and the oven, as well as making an easy no-cook snack to round out the recipes. But your active time in the kitchen will not be extensive since the recipes cook simultaneously. This week you will be enjoying a hearty stew, a juicy pork dish, and two Southwestern-inspired meals with a little heat and lots of color.

Mediterranean Layered Dip, page 49

SHOPPING LIST

5-INGREDIENT PANTRY

- *Black pepper, freshly ground*
- *Garlic, minced (2 tablespoons)*
- *Nonstick cooking spray*
- *Oil, olive (2 tablespoons)*
- *Onion, sweet (3)*
- *Salt, sea*

MEAT, POULTRY, SEAFOOD

- Bacon (6 slices)
- Beef, stewing (1 pound)
- Pork tenderloin (12 ounces)

DAIRY AND NONDAIRY SUBSTITUTES

- Cheddar cheese, shredded (1½ cups)
- Feta cheese, crumbled (½ cup)
- Sour cream (1 cup)

PRODUCE

- Bell peppers, red (2)
- Carrots (6)
- Kale (2 cups)
- Potatoes, russet (4)
- Zucchini (2)

CANNED AND JARRED

- Black beans, low-sodium (1 [15-ounce] can)
- Corn, low-sodium (1 [8¾-ounce] can)
- Great northern beans, low-sodium (3 [15-ounce] cans)
- Salsa (1½ cups)
- Tomatoes, diced, low-sodium (1 [28-ounce] can)

PANTRY

- Chili powder (1 tablespoon)
- Seasoning blend (4 teaspoons)

OTHER

- Peas, frozen (1 cup)
- Pita chips (5 ounces)
- Tortillas, corn, 3 (10-inch)

	BREAKFAST	LUNCH	DINNER	SNACK/DESSERT
DAY 1	Bacon Breakfast Cassoulet	Black Bean Chili Quesadillas	Slow Cooker Tomato and Beef Stew	Mediterranean Layered Dip
DAY 2	Bacon Breakfast Cassoulet	Slow Cooker Tomato and Beef Stew	Spice-Rubbed Pork Tenderloin	Mediterranean Layered Dip
DAY 3	Bacon Breakfast Cassoulet	Black Bean Chili Quesadillas	Spice-Rubbed Pork Tenderloin	Mediterranean Layered Dip
DAY 4	Bacon Breakfast Cassoulet	Black Bean Chili Quesadillas	Slow Cooker Tomato and Beef Stew	Mediterranean Layered Dip
DAY 5	Bacon Breakfast Cassoulet	Spice-Rubbed Pork Tenderloin	Slow Cooker Tomato and Beef Stew	Mediterranean Layered Dip

STEP-BY-STEP PREP

1. Prep all the vegetables needed for this week:
   - Cut the bell peppers into thick strips.
   - Peel the carrots and cut them into thin discs.
   - Cut the zucchini into 2-inch chunks.
   - Dice the onions.
   - Peel 2 potatoes and dice.
   - Peel 2 potatoes and shred.
2. Preheat the oven to 350°F.
3. Pan-sear the beef for the Slow Cooker Tomato and Beef Stew (page 47) and transfer it to the slow cooker with 1 cup of chopped onions, half of the prepared carrots, and the remaining ingredients for this recipe. Start the slow cooker.

4. Clean the skillet and pan-sear the pork tenderloin for the Spice-Rubbed Pork Tenderloin (page 48), then place it on the baking sheet. Add the remaining ingredients, including the remaining carrots, to the baking sheet and roast.

5. Prepare the Mediterranean Layered Dip (page 49). Divide the pita chips and place into the large section of 5 (2-compartment) containers, and divide the dip among the smaller sections of each container. Label and store in the refrigerator for up to 1 week.

6. Clean out the skillet and prepare the Black Bean Chili Quesadillas (page 46) completely using 1 cup of onion. Cut each cooled quesadilla in half and place each in a medium container. Seal, label, and store in the refrigerator for up to 4 days.

7. Chop the bacon for the Bacon Breakfast Cassoulet (page 45) and prepare the recipe completely. Spoon the mixture into 5 large containers and place 3 in the refrigerator for up to 3 days and 2 in the freezer for up to 1 month.

8. Evenly divide the vegetables for the Spice-Rubbed Pork Tenderloin among 3 large (2-compartment) containers, placing them in the large section. Cut the pork into 9 pieces and place 3 pieces in the small side of each container. Refrigerate 2 of the containers for up to 3 days and freeze 1 for up to 1 month.

9. When the stew is finished, portion it into 4 large meal prep containers and set aside to cool. Cover, label, and store 2 containers in the refrigerator for up to 3 days and 2 in the freezer for up to 1 month.

DAIRY-FREE • GLUTEN-FREE • NUT-FREE

BACON BREAKFAST CASSOULET

SERVINGS: 5 • **PREP TIME:** 15 minutes • **COOK TIME:** 19 minutes

A cassoulet is actually the container that you would cook a recipe like this in, but a skillet works just as well. Beans for breakfast might sound odd, but they are a common meal component around the world, and their protein and fiber will give you a great start to your day and keep you full for hours. For a bit of a kick, add a splash of your favorite hot sauce.

6 slices bacon, chopped

1 teaspoon olive oil

1 sweet onion, chopped

2 teaspoons minced garlic

3 cups peeled, shredded potato (about 2 large), liquid squeezed out

2 (15-ounce) cans low-sodium great northern beans, drained and rinsed

2 cups chopped fresh kale

1 teaspoon seasoning blend (your choice) or All-Purpose Spice Rub (page 173)

Sea salt

1. Heat a large skillet over medium-high heat and add the bacon. Sauté until cooked through and crispy, about 6 minutes. Using a slotted spoon, place the bacon on paper towels to drain excess fat.

2. Put the oil in the skillet and sauté the onion and garlic until softened, about 3 minutes.

3. Add the potato and sauté until lightly browned, about 5 minutes.

4. Add the beans, kale, and seasoning and sauté until the beans are heated through and the kale is wilted, about 5 minutes.

5. Stir the bacon back into the skillet and season lightly with salt. Remove from heat.

REHEATING TIP: To reheat, microwave uncovered for 30-second intervals until heated through. To reheat from frozen, thaw in the refrigerator overnight before reheating as directed.

SUBSTITUTION TIP: Shredded sweet potato and butternut squash can take the place of the potato in this dish. The added sweetness is lovely with the salty, rich bacon.

Per serving: Calories: 417; Total fat: 14g; Saturated fat: 0g; Protein: 19g; Total carbs: 56g; Fiber: 11g; Sugar: 7g; Sodium: 389mg

GLUTEN-FREE • NUT-FREE • VEGETARIAN

BLACK BEAN CHILI QUESADILLAS

SERVINGS: 3 • **PREP TIME:** 10 minutes • **COOK TIME:** 12 to 18 minutes

Quesadillas are not only delicious, but they also hold up in the refrigerator and freeze extremely well, making them the perfect meal to prep in advance. You can use whole-wheat tortillas instead of corn, but they are higher in sodium and do not stay as crispy when stored in the refrigerator for a few days.

1 (15-ounce) can low-sodium black beans, drained and rinsed

1 (8¾-ounce) can low-sodium corn, drained and rinsed

1 sweet onion, chopped

1 teaspoon minced garlic

1 tablespoon chili powder

3 (10-inch) corn tortillas

1½ cups shredded cheddar cheese

Nonstick cooking spray

1. In a medium bowl, mash the beans with a fork. Add the corn, onion, garlic, and chili powder and mix well.

2. Lay the tortillas on a clean work surface and divide the filling evenly among them, spreading it out on one-half of each tortilla about ½ inch from the edge. Sprinkle the cheese evenly over top of each and fold the other side of the tortilla over the filling, pressing to seal.

3. Heat a large skillet over medium-high heat and grease it generously with cooking spray.

4. Cook the quesadillas one at a time, flipping once halfway through, until the tortilla is golden and the cheese is melted, 4 to 6 minutes. Repeat with the remaining quesadillas.

5. Let the quesadillas cool.

REHEATING TIP: Quesadillas taste fabulous cold or hot; if eating them hot, reheat in the microwave for 30 seconds.

Per serving: Calories: 504; Total fat: 21g; Saturated fat: 6g; Protein: 25g; Total carbs: 54g; Fiber: 15g; Sugar: 8g; Sodium: 573mg

DAIRY-FREE • GLUTEN-FREE • NUT-FREE

SLOW COOKER TOMATO and BEEF STEW

SERVINGS: 4 • **PREP TIME:** 15 minutes • **COOK TIME:** 5 hours on high or 8 hours on low

Beef stew is a classic comfort food, is economical, and maintains its flavor and quality in the refrigerator or freezer. If you plan to freeze the stew, swap out sweet potatoes or butternut squash for the regular potatoes, which can get grainy and mushy when reheated from frozen. This stew is also lovely with lamb or pork instead of beef.

Nonstick cooking spray

2 teaspoons olive oil

1 pound stewing beef, trimmed

1 sweet onion, chopped

1 tablespoon minced garlic

1 (28-ounce) can low-sodium diced tomatoes

¼ cup water

3 carrots, thinly cut into rounds

2 large russet potatoes, diced

1 cup frozen peas

Sea salt

Freshly ground black pepper

1. Grease the insert of a slow cooker with cooking spray.
2. In a large skillet, heat the oil over medium-high heat. Add the beef and brown on all sides, about 10 minutes.
3. Transfer the beef to the slow cooker and add the onion, garlic, tomatoes, water, carrots, and potatoes.
4. Cover and cook on high for 5 hours or on low for 8 hours.
5. Add the peas and season with salt and pepper.

REHEATING TIP: To reheat, microwave uncovered for 30-second intervals until heated through. To reheat from frozen, thaw in the refrigerator overnight before reheating as directed.

COOKING TIP: If you do not have a slow cooker, make the stew in a stockpot on the stove. Brown the beef as directed, sauté the onion and garlic, and add the remaining ingredients. Bring to a boil, reduce the heat to low, and simmer until the stew is very tender, stirring occasionally, about 2½ hours.

Per serving: Calories: 400; Total fat: 8g; Saturated fat: 2g; Protein: 32g; Total carbs: 54g; Fiber: 11g; Sugar: 13g; Sodium: 164mg

DAIRY-FREE • GLUTEN-FREE • NUT-FREE

SPICE-RUBBED PORK TENDERLOIN

SERVINGS: 3 • **PREP TIME:** 15 minutes • **COOK TIME:** 35 minutes

Pork tenderloin is an often-overlooked protein choice, but it is reasonably priced and simple to cook, so it should be a regular addition to your diet. Pork is high in protein and vitamin B_6 and this cut is very lean, so it's low in saturated fat. This also means it can dry out when roasting, so use a digital thermometer to monitor the internal temperature to avoid overcooking it.

12 ounces pork tenderloin, trimmed and skin removed

1 tablespoon seasoning blend (your choice) or All-Purpose Spice Rub (page 173)

3 teaspoons olive oil, divided

2 red bell peppers, seeded and cut into thick strips

3 carrots, cut into thin discs

2 zucchini, cut into 2-inch chunks

Sea salt

Freshly ground black pepper

1. Preheat the oven to 350°F. Line a baking sheet with parchment paper.
2. Rub the pork tenderloin with the spice mixture, covering it evenly.
3. Heat 1 teaspoon of oil in a large skillet over medium-high heat. Brown the tenderloin well on all sides, about 5 minutes total, and transfer the tenderloin to one-quarter of the baking sheet.
4. In a large bowl, toss the bell peppers, carrots, and zucchini with the remaining 2 teaspoons of oil and season lightly with salt and black pepper.
5. Spread the vegetables on the remaining three-quarters of the baking sheet with the tenderloin and roast in the oven for 30 minutes, until the meat is cooked through to an internal temperature of 145°F and the vegetables are tender, turning once.
6. Remove the meat and vegetables from the oven and let cool.

REHEATING TIP: To reheat, microwave uncovered for 30-second intervals until heated through. To reheat from frozen, thaw in the refrigerator overnight before reheating as directed.

Per serving: Calories: 235; Total fat: 8g; Saturated fat: 1g; Protein: 27g; Total carbs: 15g; Fiber: 4g; Sugar: 10g; Sodium: 116mg

NUT-FREE • VEGETARIAN

MEDITERRANEAN LAYERED DIP

SERVINGS: 5 • **PREP TIME:** 10 minutes

Dips are a fabulous snack, and this one is both pretty and delicious, with a satisfying crunch from the pita chips. Great northern beans can be replaced with a 15-ounce can of low-sodium refried beans to save a bit of prep time.

1 (15-ounce) can low-sodium great northern beans, drained and rinsed

1 cup sour cream

1½ cups store-bought salsa or Pico de Gallo (page 179)

½ cup crumbled feta cheese

5 to 6 ounces pita chips or tortilla chips

1. Use the back of a spoon to mash the beans directly in the can after draining and rinsing them. Evenly divide the mashed beans among the small sections of 5 large (2-compartment) containers or 5 small sealable containers.

2. Layer the sour cream, salsa, and cheese over the beans, dividing each evenly. Serve with pita chips.

INGREDIENT TIP: Add chopped avocado, jalapeño peppers, roasted red pepper, or black olives to this delectable dip.

SUBSTITUTION TIP: You can use carrot or celery sticks to dip instead of pita chips.

Per serving: Calories: 308; Total fat: 15g; Saturated fat: 7g; Protein: 11g; Total carbs: 33g; Fiber: 5g; Sugar: 5g; Sodium: 553mg

CHAPTER 5

Week 5 Prep

Pumpkin Sausage Egg Casserole 55

Creamy Potato Leek Soup 56

Garam Masala Chicken Thighs with Broccoli 57

Pesto Tilapia Vegetable Packets 58

Sesame Brown Rice Treats 59

Congratulations! You made it to week five—you are now a veteran meal prepper. This week should be a breeze for you. Chicken broth, rice, spices, and frozen vegetables are easily swapped with other ingredients in these meals if you like. This week you might be trying a new culinary technique: cooking in foil or paper packets. Have fun starting your second month of five-ingredient meal prepping!

Pumpkin Sausage Egg Casserole, page 55

SHOPPING LIST

5-INGREDIENT PANTRY

- *Black pepper, freshly ground*
- *Garlic, minced (4 teaspoons)*
- *Nonstick cooking spray*
- *Oil, olive (5 tablespoons)*
- *Onion, sweet (2)*
- *Salt, sea*

MEAT, POULTRY, OR SEAFOOD

- Chicken, 3 (4-ounce) boneless, skin-on thighs
- Sausage meat (8 ounces)
- Tilapia, 3 (6-ounce) fillets

DAIRY AND NONDAIRY SUBSTITUTES

- Butter (3 tablespoons)
- Cream, heavy (whipping) (½ cup)
- Eggs, large (12)

PRODUCE

- Asparagus (1 bunch)
- Baby spinach (2 cups)
- Bell pepper, red (1)
- Broccoli (1 head)
- Broccoli slaw (6 cups)
- Cilantro, fresh (1 bunch)
- Leeks (3)
- Potatoes, russet, large (3)

CANNED AND JARRED

- Pesto (3 tablespoons)

PANTRY

- Chicken broth, low-sodium (4½ cups)
- Garam masala spice (1 tablespoon)
- Marshmallows, mini (4 cups)
- Nutmeg, ground (¼ teaspoon)
- Rice, white (¾ cup)
- Rice cereal, brown, puffed (4 cups)
- Sesame seeds, toasted (2 tablespoons)
- Vanilla extract, pure (1 teaspoon)

OTHER

- Pumpkin, frozen (2 cups)

	BREAKFAST	LUNCH	DINNER	SNACK/DESSERT
DAY 1	Pumpkin Sausage Egg Casserole	Creamy Potato Leek Soup	Pesto Tilapia Vegetable Packets	Sesame Brown Rice Treats
DAY 2	Pumpkin Sausage Egg Casserole	Creamy Potato Leek Soup	Pesto Tilapia Vegetable Packets	Sesame Brown Rice Treats
DAY 3	Pumpkin Sausage Egg Casserole	Pesto Tilapia Vegetable Packets	Garam Masala Chicken Thighs with Broccoli	Sesame Brown Rice Treats
DAY 4	Pumpkin Sausage Egg Casserole	Creamy Potato Leek Soup	Garam Masala Chicken Thighs with Broccoli	Sesame Brown Rice Treats
DAY 5	Pumpkin Sausage Egg Casserole	Creamy Potato Leek Soup	Garam Masala Chicken Thighs with Broccoli	Sesame Brown Rice Treats

STEP-BY-STEP PREP

1. Preheat the oven to 350°F.
2. Prepare all the vegetables for the recipes:
   - Chop the pumpkin into about ½-inch chunks. Thaw it at room temperature for 15 minutes to make it easier to cut.
   - Chop the bell pepper.
   - Chop the onions.
   - Slice and thoroughly clean the leeks.
   - Peel and dice the potatoes.
   - Cut the broccoli into small florets.
   - Trim the asparagus and cut into 3-inch pieces.

3. Prepare the Pumpkin Sausage Egg Casserole (page 55) completely, using 1 cup of the chopped onion, and bake.

4. Prepare the Creamy Potato Leek Soup (page 56) completely, using the remaining chopped onion.

5. While simmering the soup, prepare the Sesame Brown Rice Treats (page 59) completely. Set aside to cool.

6. Portion the soup among 4 large meal prep containers and seal, label, and store in the refrigerator for up to 5 days or in the freezer for up to 1 month.

7. Remove the casserole from the oven and transfer the portions to 5 medium containers. Seal, label, and store 3 in the refrigerator for up to 3 days and 2 in the freezer for up to 1 month.

8. Set the oven temperature to 425°F.

9. Pan-sear the chicken for the Garam Masala Chicken Thighs with Broccoli (page 57) and arrange the ingredients on the baking sheet. Place in the oven to roast.

10. Prepare the Pesto Tilapia Vegetable Packets (page 58) while the chicken thighs are roasting. When the chicken is done, remove from the oven and place the tilapia packets in the oven.

11. Make the rice for the chicken thigh recipe.

12. Portion the chicken thigh recipe into 3 large (3-compartment) meal prep containers, using one-third of the container for each component. Seal, label, and store 1 in the refrigerator for up to 3 days and 2 in the freezer for up to 1 month.

13. Portion the tilapia recipe into 3 large (2-compartment) containers, placing the fish in the smaller section and the vegetables in the larger section and pouring the juices on top of the fish. Seal, label, and store in the refrigerator for up to 5 days.

14. When the Sesame Brown Rice Treats are cool, place 2 squares each into 5 medium containers, label, and refrigerate for up to 1 week.

DAIRY-FREE • GLUTEN-FREE • NUT-FREE

PUMPKIN SAUSAGE EGG CASSEROLE

MAKES: 5 • **PREP TIME:** 15 minutes • **COOK TIME:** 56 minutes

Egg casseroles are one of the simplest dishes to make when you want a no-fuss meal for breakfast, lunch, or dinner. You often see pumpkin in sweet desserts, but this bright fruit is a common ingredient in savory stews, casseroles, and soups in the Middle East and North Africa.

Nonstick cooking spray

2 teaspoons olive oil

8 ounces sausage meat, removed from the casings

2 cups chopped frozen pumpkin

1 red bell pepper, seeded and chopped

1 sweet onion, chopped

2 teaspoons minced garlic

2 cups fresh baby spinach

12 large eggs

¼ teaspoon sea salt

⅛ teaspoon freshly ground black pepper

1. Preheat the oven to 350°F. Line a 9-inch square baking dish with parchment paper and grease with cooking spray.
2. In a large skillet, heat the oil over medium-high heat and sauté the sausage until cooked through, about 5 minutes.
3. Add the pumpkin, bell pepper, onion, and garlic and sauté until the vegetables are tender, about 6 minutes.
4. Transfer the mixture to the baking dish. Add the spinach, stirring to combine, then spread the mixture evenly.
5. In a medium bowl, whisk together the eggs, salt, and black pepper until well combined. Pour the eggs into the baking dish and tap the dish lightly on the counter to disperse the eggs.
6. Bake until the casserole is just cooked through and lightly browned on top, about 45 minutes.
7. Remove the casserole from the oven, cool for 10 minutes, and cut into 5 portions.

REHEATING TIP: To reheat, microwave uncovered for 45 seconds. To reheat from frozen, thaw in the refrigerator overnight before reheating as directed. This meal can also be eaten cold from the refrigerator.

Per serving: Calories: 390; Total fat: 27g; Saturated fat: 9g; Protein: 23g; Total carbs: 11g; Fiber: 2g; Sugar: 6g; Sodium: 521mg

GLUTEN-FREE • NUT-FREE • VEGETARIAN

CREAMY POTATO LEEK SOUP

SERVINGS: 4 • **PREP TIME:** 15 minutes • **COOK TIME:** 27 to 32 minutes

Potato leek soup is creamy, slightly sweet, and a stick-to-the-ribs kind of meal. The nice part about making this elegant soup is that it is equally delicious hot or cold. Cold potato leek soup is called vichyssoise, and it is a much-loved French staple. If you enjoy a richer creation, top the soup with chopped bacon and a generous sprinkling of cheddar cheese.

1 tablespoon olive oil

3 leeks, white and light green parts, thinly sliced

1 sweet onion, chopped

2 teaspoons minced garlic

4 cups low-sodium chicken broth

3 large russet potatoes, diced

½ cup heavy (whipping) cream

¼ teaspoon ground nutmeg

Sea salt

Freshly ground black pepper

1. In a large saucepan, heat the oil over medium-high heat.
2. Sauté the leeks, onion, and garlic until the vegetables are softened, about 7 minutes.
3. Add the broth and potatoes and bring to a boil.
4. Reduce the heat to low and simmer until the potatoes are tender, 20 to 25 minutes.
5. Remove the soup from the heat and use an immersion blender to puree until smooth, or transfer the soup to a food processor and puree in batches.
6. Add the cream and nutmeg and season the soup with salt and pepper.

REHEATING TIP: To reheat, microwave uncovered for 30-second intervals until heated through.

COOKING TIP: If freezing the soup, leave the cream out and add it when you reheat to serve.

Per serving: Calories: 460; Total fat: 16g; Saturated fat: 8g; Protein: 13g; Total carbs: 69g; Fiber: 6g; Sugar: 10g; Sodium: 117mg

DAIRY-FREE • GLUTEN-FREE • NUT-FREE

GARAM MASALA CHICKEN THIGHS with BROCCOLI

SERVINGS: 3 • **PREP TIME:** 10 minutes • **COOK TIME:** 36 minutes

Garam masala is an Indian spice blend of black pepper, cinnamon, nutmeg, coriander, cloves, cardamom, and cumin. These spices are thought to improve digestion and metabolism. Serve with hot sauce, yogurt, and naan bread for an authentic Middle Eastern meal.

3 (4-ounce) boneless, skinless chicken thighs

1 tablespoon garam masala spice

3 tablespoons olive oil, divided

1 head broccoli, cut into small florets

Sea salt

¾ cup white rice

1½ cups water

1 tablespoon chopped fresh cilantro

1. Preheat the oven to 425°F. Line a baking sheet with parchment paper.

2. Rub the chicken thighs all over with the garam masala. In a large skillet, heat 1 tablespoon of oil over medium-high heat and pan-sear the chicken thighs until browned, turning once halfway through, about 6 minutes total.

3. Transfer the chicken to one-half of the baking sheet. Place the chicken in the oven and roast for 15 minutes.

4. In a large bowl, toss together the remaining 2 tablespoons of oil and the broccoli and season lightly with salt. After 15 minutes, take the chicken out of the oven and arrange the broccoli on the other side of the baking sheet.

5. Roast the chicken and broccoli until the chicken is cooked through and the broccoli is tender, about 15 minutes more.

6. While the chicken is cooking, stir together the rice and water in a medium saucepan over medium-high heat and bring to a boil. Reduce the heat to low, cover, and simmer until the liquid is absorbed, about 20 minutes. Top with the cilantro.

REHEATING TIP: To reheat, microwave uncovered for 30-second intervals until heated through. To reheat from frozen, thaw in the refrigerator overnight before reheating as directed.

Per serving: Calories: 511; Total fat: 19g; Saturated fat: 3g; Protein: 31g; Total carbs: 54g; Fiber: 7g; Sugar: 4g; Sodium: 177mg

GLUTEN-FREE

PESTO TILAPIA VEGETABLE PACKETS

SERVINGS: 3 • **PREP TIME:** 10 minutes • **COOK TIME:** 15 to 18 minutes

Cooking en papillote is a culinary technique used to cook delicate ingredients, such as fish, so that they stay moist in the trapped steam. En papillote means "in paper or parchment," and you can use this material to make your packets because kitchen parchment is processed so that the surface is sturdy and will not let liquid escape.

Nonstick cooking spray

6 cups broccoli slaw

1 bunch asparagus, woody ends removed and stalks cut into 3-inch pieces

Sea salt

Freshly ground black pepper

3 (6-ounce) tilapia fillets

3 tablespoons store-bought pesto or Traditional Basil Pesto (page 177)

½ cup low-sodium chicken broth

1. Preheat the oven to 425°F.
2. Cut 3 (12-by-18-inch) sheets of aluminum foil. Spread the foil on a clean work surface and spray each piece lightly with the cooking spray.
3. Evenly divide the broccoli slaw and asparagus among the foil pieces, piling the vegetables in a mound in the middle. Season the vegetables with salt and pepper. Turn up the edges of the foil.
4. Place a fish fillet on top of each pile of vegetables and spread each fillet evenly with the pesto. Drizzle the fish and vegetables with the chicken broth.
5. Fold the edges of the foil together to create a packet and crimp to seal. Place the packets in a 9-by-13-inch baking dish or on a baking sheet.
6. Bake until the vegetables and fish are tender, 15 to 18 minutes.
7. Remove the packets from the oven and set aside to cool for 30 minutes.

REHEATING TIP: To reheat, microwave uncovered for 30-second intervals until heated through.

COOKING TIP: When opening the packets, be careful of the very hot steam that will be released.

Per serving: Calories: 330; Total fat: 13g; Saturated fat: 3g; Protein: 43g; Total carbs: 16g; Fiber: 6g; Sugar: 4g; Sodium: 269mg

GLUTEN-FREE • NUT-FREE • VEGETARIAN

SESAME BROWN RICE TREATS

SERVINGS: 5 • **PREP TIME:** 10 minutes • **COOK TIME:** 5 minutes

Yes, these are an enhanced version of Rice Krispies Treats, and the sesame seeds add a much deeper flavor profile. If you are not a fan of sesame seeds, you can certainly leave them out or replace them with something else such as mini chocolate chips, dried cranberries, or chopped nuts. These treats freeze well, so if they are your snack of choice, double the recipe and store extra portions in the freezer for up to 2 months.

Nonstick cooking spray

3 tablespoons butter

4 cups mini marshmallows

1 teaspoon pure vanilla extract

4 cups puffed brown rice cereal

2 tablespoons toasted sesame seeds

1. Lightly spray an 8-inch square baking dish with cooking spray.
2. In a medium stockpot, melt the butter over medium heat. Add the marshmallows and vanilla and stir until the marshmallows are completely melted, about 5 minutes.
3. Add the puffed rice cereal and mix well. Transfer the mixture to the baking dish and press firmly into the bottom of the dish. Sprinkle the sesame seeds over top and press the seeds firmly into the surface.
4. Refrigerate until firm, about 2 hours.
5. Cut the treats into 10 pieces.

SUBSTITUTION TIP: Puffed wheat, quinoa, kamut, or any other similar cereal works well for these treats, and each type adds a different texture and taste.

Per serving: Calories: 127; Total fat: 4g; Saturated fat: 2g; Protein: 1g; Total carbs: 22g; Fiber: 0g; Sugar: 12g; Sodium: 53mg

CHAPTER 6

Week 6 Prep

Banana Baked Oatmeal 65

Mediterranean Turkey Bowls 66

Split Pea Root Vegetable Soup 67

Honey Sesame Salmon with Squash 68

Almond Quinoa Pudding 69

This week's menu is fiber-friendly and includes variations of familiar dishes such as baked oatmeal instead of porridge and a quinoa pudding instead of the classic rice version. As with most other meal prep menus so far, this week has a shopping list under 25 items and the active kitchen time totals about two and a half hours.

Honey Sesame Salmon with Squash, page 68

SHOPPING LIST

5-INGREDIENT PANTRY

- *Black pepper, freshly ground*
- *Garlic, minced (1 tablespoon)*
- *Nonstick cooking spray*
- *Oil, olive (3 tablespoons)*
- *Onion, sweet (1)*
- *Salt, sea*

MEAT, POULTRY, OR SEAFOOD

- Salmon, 3 (4-ounce) fillets
- Turkey, boneless, skinless breast (12 ounces)

DAIRY AND NONDAIRY SUBSTITUTES

- Almond milk, sweetened, vanilla (3½ cups)
- Eggs, large (2)
- Feta cheese, crumbled (½ cup)

PRODUCE

- Bananas (3)
- Bell peppers, mixed colors (4)
- Butternut squash (1)
- Carrots (3)
- Celery (3 stalks)
- Scallion (1)

CANNED AND JARRED

- Greek dressing (6 tablespoons)
- Honey (3 tablespoons)
- Maple syrup (¼ cup)

PANTRY

- Almonds, unsalted, sliced (¼ cup)
- Baking powder (1 teaspoon)
- Chicken broth, low-sodium (6 cups)
- Cinnamon, ground (¼ teaspoon)
- Farro (¾ cup)
- Oats, rolled (2½ cups)
- Peas, split, dry (12 ounces)
- Quinoa, dry (1 cup)
- Sesame seeds, toasted (2 tablespoons)
- Thyme, dried (2 teaspoons)

	BREAKFAST	LUNCH	DINNER	SNACK/DESSERT
DAY 1	Banana Baked Oatmeal	Mediterranean Turkey Bowls	Honey Sesame Salmon with Squash	Almond Quinoa Pudding
DAY 2	Banana Baked Oatmeal	Split Pea Root Vegetable Soup	Honey Sesame Salmon with Squash	Almond Quinoa Pudding
DAY 3	Banana Baked Oatmeal	Split Pea Root Vegetable Soup	Honey Sesame Salmon with Squash	Almond Quinoa Pudding
DAY 4	Banana Baked Oatmeal	Split Pea Root Vegetable Soup	Mediterranean Turkey Bowls	Almond Quinoa Pudding
DAY 5	Banana Baked Oatmeal	Mediterranean Turkey Bowls	Split Pea Root Vegetable Soup	Almond Quinoa Pudding

STEP-BY-STEP PREP

1. Preheat the oven to 350°F.
2. Make the Banana Baked Oatmeal (page 65) completely and place it in the oven to bake.
3. Cook the farro for the Mediterranean Turkey Bowls (page 66) and evenly divide the cooked farro among 3 large (2-compartment) meal prep containers, spooning it into the small side.

4. Prepare the vegetables for all the recipes:
   - Dice the bell peppers.
   - Chop the celery stalks.
   - Chop the onion.
   - Dice the carrots.
   - Peel the butternut squash and cut into 1-inch chunks.
   - Thinly slice the scallion.
5. Dice the turkey for the turkey bowls and sauté it with the peppers (following the recipe directions). Evenly divide the turkey and pepper mixture among the containers, placing it in the large side, and top each turkey portion with about 3 tablespoons of feta. Seal, label, and store 1 of the containers in the refrigerator for up to 3 days and 2 in the freezer for up to 1 month.
6. Prepare the Split Pea Root Vegetable Soup (page 67) recipe completely.
7. Remove the baked oatmeal from the oven and place the portions into 5 medium containers. Seal, label, and store 3 containers in the refrigerator for up to 3 days and 2 in the freezer for up to 1 month.
8. Increase the oven temperature to 400°F.
9. Prepare the Honey Sesame Salmon with Squash (page 68) and place in the oven to bake.
10. Prepare the Almond Quinoa Pudding (page 69) recipe completely. Portion into 5 medium containers, label, and refrigerate for up to 1 week.
11. Transfer the Split Pea Root Vegetable Soup to 4 large containers. Seal, label, and store 2 containers in the refrigerator for up to 3 days and 2 in the freezer for up to 1 month.
12. When the salmon recipe is finished cooking, evenly divide the squash into the large side of 3 large (2-compartment) meal prep containers and place 1 piece of salmon into the small side of each container. Top with scallions and seal, label, and store in the refrigerator for up to 3 days.

DAIRY-FREE • GLUTEN-FREE • NUT-FREE • VEGETARIAN

BANANA BAKED OATMEAL

SERVINGS: 5 • **PREP TIME:** 10 minutes • **COOK TIME:** 25 to 30 minutes

Cooked oatmeal is a popular choice for breakfast in many households because it is inexpensive and can be thrown together with little effort. Did you know you can also bake it to create moist, delicious squares that are ideal for keeping in the refrigerator for meals later in the week? You can eat baked oatmeal cold, like a large, soft granola bar, or warm it up plain or with a splash of milk.

Nonstick cooking spray

3 ripe bananas

2 large eggs

1½ cups sweetened vanilla almond milk

2½ cups rolled oats

1 teaspoon baking powder

¼ teaspoon sea salt

1. Preheat the oven to 350°F. Lightly grease a 9-inch round baking dish with cooking spray.
2. In a large bowl, mash the bananas with a fork or potato masher until very few lumps remain, then whisk in the eggs and almond milk until well blended.
3. Add the oats, baking powder, and salt and stir to combine.
4. Spoon the mixture into the baking dish, smoothing the top evenly.
5. Bake for 25 to 30 minutes, or until a knife inserted in the middle comes out clean.
6. Let cool on a wire rack for about 1 hour.
7. Cut the oatmeal into 5 equal pieces.

REHEATING TIP: Eat the oatmeal cold or reheat by microwaving uncovered for 30-second intervals until heated through. To reheat from frozen, thaw in the refrigerator overnight before reheating as directed.

Per serving: Calories: 423; Total fat: 8g; Saturated fat: 1g; Protein: 17g; Total carbs: 73g; Fiber: 10g; Sugar: 13g; Sodium: 193mg

NUT-FREE

MEDITERRANEAN TURKEY BOWLS

SERVINGS: 3 • **PREP TIME:** 15 minutes • **COOK TIME:** 20 minutes

This is a perfect dish to make if you have leftover cooked turkey because it will save prep time. A good tip for when you do prepare a large whole bird is to strip all the meat from the bones and store it in one- or two-cup portions in the freezer. Just take out a bag when you want to make a recipe like this one and thaw it in the refrigerator overnight before your cooking day. This recipe would require about 4 cups of cooked turkey.

¾ cup farro

2 cups water

12 ounces boneless, skinless turkey breast, diced into 1-inch cubes

Sea salt

Freshly ground black pepper

1 tablespoon olive oil

4 medium bell peppers, mixed colors, seeded and diced

6 tablespoons store-bought Greek dressing

½ cup crumbled feta cheese

1. In a medium saucepan, combine the farro and water and place it over medium-high heat. Bring to a boil, then reduce the heat, cover, and simmer until the grains are tender and the water is absorbed, about 20 minutes.
2. While the farro is cooking, lightly season the turkey with salt and black pepper.
3. Heat the oil in a large skillet and sauté the turkey until cooked through and lightly browned, about 15 minutes.
4. Add the bell peppers to the skillet and sauté until tender, about 5 minutes.
5. Remove the skillet from the heat and add the Greek dressing. Top with the cheese.

REHEATING TIP: To reheat, microwave uncovered for 30-second intervals until heated through. To reheat from frozen, thaw in the refrigerator overnight before reheating as directed.

Per serving: Calories: 435; Total fat: 15g; Saturated fat: 5g; Protein: 36g; Total carbs: 42g; Fiber: 8g; Sugar: 12g; Sodium: 517mg

DAIRY-FREE • GLUTEN-FREE • NUT-FREE

SPLIT PEA ROOT VEGETABLE SOUP

SERVINGS: 4 • **PREP TIME:** 15 minutes • **COOK TIME:** 54 minutes

Split pea soup is a lovely choice for dinner or lunch because it is satisfying without making you feel bloated or too full. Split peas are an excellent source of protein, low in fat, and very high in fiber. They can help stabilize blood sugar, support digestion, and reduce the risk of cardiovascular disease and cancer. Perfect for any time of year, this soup is an especially good light option for cold weather.

1 tablespoon olive oil

3 celery stalks, chopped

1 sweet onion, chopped

1 tablespoon minced garlic

6 cups low-sodium chicken broth

12 ounces split peas, drained and rinsed

3 carrots, diced

2 teaspoons dried thyme

Sea salt

Freshly ground black pepper

1. In a medium stockpot, heat the olive oil over medium-high heat.
2. Add the celery, onion, and garlic and sauté until softened, about 4 minutes.
3. Add the chicken broth and split peas and bring the soup to a boil.
4. Partially cover, reduce the heat to low, and simmer until the peas are al dente, about 30 minutes.
5. Add the carrots and thyme and simmer until the carrots are tender and the soup is thick, about 20 minutes.
6. Remove the soup from the heat and season lightly with salt and pepper.

REHEATING TIP: To reheat, microwave uncovered for 30-second intervals until heated through. To reheat from frozen, thaw in the refrigerator overnight before reheating as directed.

Per serving: Calories: 438; Total fat: 7g; Saturated fat: 1g; Protein: 29g; Total carbs: 70g; Fiber: 24g; Sugar: 14g; Sodium: 170mg

DAIRY-FREE • GLUTEN-FREE • NUT-FREE

HONEY SESAME SALMON with SQUASH

SERVINGS: 3 • **PREP TIME:** 15 minutes • **COOK TIME:** 15 minutes

Honey adds a luscious caramelized surface to salmon that tastes incredible with this assertive fish. The honey topping also keeps the fish moist and reheats well when you enjoy this meal throughout the week. If you like a more savory glaze, add 1 teaspoon of soy sauce to the honey before topping the fish.

3 (4-ounce) salmon fillets

Sea salt

3 teaspoons olive oil, divided

3 tablespoons honey

2 tablespoons toasted sesame seeds

1 butternut squash, peeled, seeded, and cut into 1-inch chunks

Freshly ground black pepper

1 scallion, white and green parts, thinly sliced

1. Preheat the oven to 400°F. Line a baking sheet with parchment paper.
2. Season the salmon lightly on both sides with salt.
3. In a large skillet, heat 1 teaspoon of oil over medium-high heat. Pan-sear the salmon on both sides, turning once halfway through, about 3 minutes total. Place the fillets on one-quarter of the baking sheet and evenly spread the honey on each. Then sprinkle the fillets with sesame seeds.
4. In a large bowl, combine the squash with the remaining 2 teaspoons of oil. Lightly season the squash with salt and pepper and place on the remaining three-quarters of the baking sheet.
5. Bake for 10 to 12 minutes, or until the fish flakes easily with a fork.
6. Remove the fish and squash from the oven. Divide into 3 equal portions and top each with the sliced scallions.

REHEATING TIP: To reheat, microwave uncovered for 30-second intervals until heated through.

Per serving: Calories: 406; Total fat: 14g; Saturated fat: 2g; Protein: 28g; Total carbs: 46g; Fiber: 6g; Sugar: 22g; Sodium: 95mg

DAIRY-FREE • GLUTEN-FREE • VEGAN

ALMOND QUINOA PUDDING

SERVINGS: 5 • **PREP TIME:** 5 minutes • **COOK TIME:** 20 minutes

Rice pudding is probably a more familiar version of this grain-based dessert, but quinoa is delightful as well. Quinoa creates a creamier, more delicate texture than rice and has a pleasing nutty flavor. This snack is wonderful warm or cold but if you are reheating it, you might want to add a little extra almond milk to thin the texture.

- **2 cups sweetened vanilla almond milk**
- **1 cup quinoa, rinsed**
- **¼ teaspoon ground cinnamon**
- Pinch sea salt
- **¼ cup maple syrup**
- **¼ cup sliced unsalted almonds**

1. In a large saucepan, stir together the almond milk, quinoa, cinnamon, and salt over medium heat. Bring the mixture to a boil, stirring frequently, then reduce the heat to low and simmer until the liquid is absorbed, about 20 minutes.

2. Remove the pudding from the heat and add the maple syrup. Divide into 5 equal portions and top each with the sliced almonds.

Per serving: Calories: 251; Total fat: 7g; Saturated fat: 1g; Protein: 7g; Total carbs: 40g; Fiber: 4g; Sugar: 16g; Sodium: 64mg

CHAPTER 7

Week 7 Prep

Mediterranean Breakfast Wraps 75

Wheat Berry Harvest Salad 76

Pecan-Crusted Pork Chops with Mashed Potatoes 77

Sheet-Pan Chicken Parmesan 78

Pumpkin Pie Tofu "Milkshake" 79

This week features a breakfast wrap with classic flavors, a hearty salad, two entrées with familiar flavors and ingredients, and a luscious dessert-themed smoothie. Similar to most other weeks so far, the shopping list is under 25 items, maybe even fewer if you already have some ingredients in your pantry. If you want to swap out any meals for something you loved in the previous six weeks, just adjust the shopping list and prep schedule accordingly.

Wheat Berry Harvest Salad, page 76

SHOPPING LIST

5-INGREDIENT PANTRY

- *Black pepper, freshly ground*
- *Garlic, minced (1 teaspoon)*
- *Nonstick cooking spray*
- *Oil, olive (4 tablespoons)*
- *Salt, sea*

MEAT, POULTRY, OR SEAFOOD

- Chicken, 4 (4-ounce) boneless, skinless breasts
- Pork, 3 (4-ounce) boneless loin chops

DAIRY AND NONDAIRY SUBSTITUTES

- Butter (2 tablespoons)
- Eggs, large (11)
- Feta cheese (3 ounces)
- Milk, 2 percent (5 cups)
- Mozzarella cheese, shredded (1 cup)
- Tofu, extra-firm (1 [14-ounce] package)

PRODUCE

- Baby spinach (4 cups)
- Carrots (4)
- Parsnips (4)
- Potatoes, russet, large (3)
- Sweet potatoes (2)

CANNED AND JARRED

- Balsamic dressing (⅓ cup)
- Maple syrup (10 tablespoons)
- Marinara sauce, low-sodium (1 [12-ounce] jar)
- Pumpkin puree (1 [28-ounce] can)
- Sun-dried tomatoes, chopped (5 tablespoons)

PANTRY

- Cranberries, dried (½ cup)
- Pecans, roasted, finely chopped (¾ cup)
- Pecans, roasted, unsalted, chopped (½ cup)
- Pumpkin pie spice (1¼ teaspoons)
- Wheat berries (1 cup)

OTHER

- Tortillas, whole-wheat, 5 (8-inch)

	BREAKFAST	LUNCH	DINNER	SNACK/DESSERT
DAY 1	Mediterranean Breakfast Wrap	Wheat Berry Harvest Salad	Sheet-Pan Chicken Parmesan	Pumpkin Pie Tofu "Milkshake"
DAY 2	Mediterranean Breakfast Wrap	Wheat Berry Harvest Salad	Pecan-Crusted Pork Chops with Mashed Potatoes	Pumpkin Pie Tofu "Milkshake"
DAY 3	Mediterranean Breakfast Wrap	Pecan-Crusted Pork Chops with Mashed Potatoes	Sheet-Pan Chicken Parmesan	Pumpkin Pie Tofu "Milkshake"
DAY 4	Mediterranean Breakfast Wrap	Wheat Berry Harvest Salad	Sheet-Pan Chicken Parmesan	Pumpkin Pie Tofu "Milkshake"
DAY 5	Mediterranean Breakfast Wrap	Sheet-Pan Chicken Parmesan	Pecan-Crusted Pork Chops with Mashed Potatoes	Pumpkin Pie Tofu "Milkshake"

STEP-BY-STEP PREP

THE NIGHT BEFORE YOUR COOKING DAY

1. Place 1 cup of wheat berries and 3 cups of water in a medium container, seal, and soak overnight in the refrigerator.

ON YOUR COOKING DAY

1. Take out all the vegetables required for the week:
    - Peel and dice the sweet potatoes, russet potatoes, carrots, and parsnips.

2. Scoop the pumpkin puree for the Pumpkin Pie Tofu "Milkshake" (page 79) into 2 ice cube trays and place the trays in the freezer. Spread the cubed tofu on a small baking sheet and place in the freezer.

3. Place the liquid ingredients for the milkshake in 5 medium meal prep containers, seal, label, and store in the refrigerator for up to 1 week.

4. Preheat the oven to 400°F.

5. Cook the wheat berries for the Wheat Berry Harvest Salad (page 76).

6. Roast the sweet potatoes for the Wheat Berry Harvest Salad.

7. Evenly divide the frozen pumpkin and tofu for the smoothies into 5 medium sealable bags. Seal, label, and store the bags in the freezer for up to 1 month.

8. Make the Mediterranean Breakfast Wraps (page 75) completely. Wrap them in foil, label, and refrigerate for up to 5 days or freeze for up to 1 month.

9. When the wheat berries and sweet potato are cooked, complete the harvest salad recipe. Portion the salad into 3 large meal prep containers and seal, label, and store in the refrigerator for up to 5 days.

10. Coat the pork chops for the Pecan-Crusted Pork Chops with Mashed Potatoes (page 77) and place them in the oven to roast. Put the potatoes on to boil for the mashed potatoes.

11. While the pork chops are roasting, prepare the Sheet-Pan Chicken Parmesan (page 78) recipe completely. Place the chicken in the oven when the pork chops are finished roasting.

12. Drain the potatoes and mash as directed.

13. Transfer the pork chops to one side of 3 (2-compartment) containers. Evenly divide the mashed potatoes among the empty compartments. Set the containers uncovered in the refrigerator to cool completely. When cool, cover the containers, label, and store 2 in the refrigerator for up to 3 days and 1 in the freezer for up to 1 month.

14. When the chicken Parmesan is finished cooking, transfer the chicken to one side of 4 large (2-compartment) containers and place the vegetables on the other side. Place the containers uncovered in the refrigerator to cool. When cool, cover the containers, label, and store 2 in the refrigerator for up to 3 days and 2 in the freezer for up to 1 month.

NUT-FREE • VEGETARIAN

MEDITERRANEAN BREAKFAST WRAPS

SERVINGS: 5 • **PREP TIME:** 15 minutes • **COOK TIME:** 6 minutes

This breakfast wrap is similar to spanakopita minus the phyllo dough, but still contains the other traditional ingredients wrapped in wholesome whole-wheat tortillas, so it is lower in fat and calories. The scrambled egg base and rich sun-dried tomatoes boost the flavor and pair beautifully with the spinach and feta.

2 teaspoons olive oil

4 cups fresh baby spinach

1 teaspoon minced garlic

10 large eggs

5 (8-inch) whole-wheat tortillas

10 tablespoons feta cheese

5 tablespoons chopped sun-dried tomatoes

Sea salt

Freshly ground black pepper

1. In a large skillet, heat the oil over medium-high heat. Sauté the spinach and garlic until tender, about 4 minutes.

2. While the spinach is cooking, whisk the eggs in a medium bowl.

3. Pour the eggs into the skillet and scramble until the eggs are just cooked through, about 2 minutes. Remove the skillet from the heat.

4. Place the tortillas on a clean work surface and evenly divide the egg and spinach mixture, cheese, and sun-dried tomatoes among each. Season lightly with salt and pepper.

5. Fold the side of each tortilla closest to you over the filling, then fold the right and left sides over that side and roll the tortilla away from you to form a sealed packet.

REHEATING TIP: To reheat, unwrap and microwave in 30-second intervals until heated through. If reheating from frozen, place the wrap on a plate and microwave on defrost for 2 to 3 minutes, turning several times. Then unwrap and microwave for 30-second intervals until heated through.

Per serving: Calories: 353; Total fat: 20g; Saturated fat: 8g; Protein: 21g; Total carbs: 23g; Fiber: 5g; Sugar: 4g; Sodium: 531mg

DAIRY-FREE • VEGAN

WHEAT BERRY HARVEST SALAD

SERVINGS: 3 • **PREP TIME:** 20 minutes • **COOK TIME:** 50 minutes

Wheat berries might be an unfamiliar ingredient to you, but the satisfying chewy texture and the nutty, slightly sweet taste should win you over. This grain holds up very well when cooked, so it is an ideal choice for meal prep. Wheat berries are high in fiber, protein, iron, and magnesium while being low in calories and fat. Since you are soaking them, look for hard red or white wheat berries because they are higher in protein.

1 cup wheat berries, soaked overnight in 3 cups water

1½ cups water

2 sweet potatoes, peeled and diced

1 tablespoon olive oil

½ cup roasted unsalted pecans, chopped

½ cup dried cranberries

⅓ cup store-bought balsamic dressing or Simple Herbed Balsamic Dressing (page 174)

Sea salt

1. Preheat the oven to 400°F. Line a half baking sheet with parchment paper.
2. Drain the wheat berries and combine them with the 1½ cups of water in a large saucepan. Bring to a boil over medium-high heat, then reduce the heat to low, partially cover, and simmer until the liquid is absorbed, about 35 minutes.
3. While the wheat berries are cooking, spread the sweet potatoes on the baking sheet and drizzle with the oil. Roast until lightly browned and tender, about 25 minutes. Remove the potatoes from the oven.
4. After 35 minutes, remove the wheat berries from the heat and let stand for 15 minutes with the lid on. Transfer the wheat berries to a large bowl.
5. Add the sweet potatoes, pecans, cranberries, and dressing to the wheat berries. Season with salt.

INGREDIENT TIP: Add crumbled feta or goat cheese to boost the flavor of this filling dish and add protein. A sweeter dressing is also lovely when combined with the nuts and dried fruit, so try a lemon poppyseed or raspberry vinaigrette.

Per serving: Calories: 457; Total fat: 26g; Saturated fat: 3g; Protein: 7g; Total carbs: 54g; Fiber: 8g; Sugar: 16g; Sodium: 259mg

GLUTEN-FREE

PECAN-CRUSTED PORK CHOPS *with* MASHED POTATOES

SERVINGS: 3 • **PREP TIME:** 15 minutes • **COOK TIME:** 30 minutes

Nut crusts provide a protective coating for lean proteins that can otherwise dry out in a hot oven. Rather than chopping the nuts, place the pecans in a plastic freezer bag and crush them with a rolling pin.

1 large egg

1 tablespoon water

¾ cup finely chopped pecans

3 (4-ounce) boneless pork loin chops, trimmed

Nonstick cooking spray

3 large russet potatoes, peeled and diced into 1-inch pieces

2 tablespoons butter

Sea salt

Freshly ground black pepper

1. Preheat the oven to 400°F. Line a 9-by-13-inch baking dish with parchment paper.

2. In a small bowl, whisk together the egg and water. Spread the pecans on a small plate next to the egg mixture.

3. Dredge the pork chops in the egg mixture and then the pecans to coat them evenly.

4. Place the pork chops in the baking dish and grease them lightly with cooking spray. Cover the baking dish with foil and bake the pork for 20 minutes. Then remove the foil and bake for 10 minutes more or until cooked through and lightly golden.

5. While the pork is cooking, place the potatoes in a large saucepan and cover with cold water by about 1 inch. Bring the potatoes to a boil over high heat, then reduce the heat to low and simmer until fork-tender, about 20 minutes.

6. Remove the potatoes from the heat, drain, and mash with a potato masher. Add the butter and season with salt and pepper.

REHEATING TIP: To reheat, microwave uncovered for 30-second intervals until heated through. To reheat from frozen, thaw the container in the refrigerator overnight before reheating as directed.

Per serving: Calories: 548; Total fat: 28g; Saturated fat: 13g; Protein: 32g; Total carbs: 42g; Fiber: 5g; Sugar: 2g; Sodium: 130mg

GLUTEN-FREE • NUT-FREE

SHEET-PAN CHICKEN PARMESAN

SERVINGS: 4 • **PREP TIME:** 15 minutes • **COOK TIME:** 29 to 34 minutes

This lighter version of chicken Parmesan is not breaded, so it will hold well for the week without getting soggy. The accompanying root vegetables are filling, and they become sweet and tender when roasted. You can pair the chicken with classic pasta and marinara sauce, but if you prefer butter on your pasta, just follow the directions for the side dish in Paprika Chicken with Butter Noodles (page 108) and change your shopping list.

4 carrots, peeled and diced into ½-inch chunks

4 parsnips, peeled and diced into ½-inch chunks

2 tablespoons olive oil, divided

Sea salt

Freshly ground black pepper

4 (4-ounce) boneless, skinless chicken breasts, pounded to ½-inch thickness

1 (12-ounce) jar low-sodium marinara sauce

1 cup shredded mozzarella cheese

1. Preheat the oven to 400°F. Line a baking sheet with parchment paper.
2. In a medium bowl, toss together the carrots, parsnips, and 1 tablespoon of oil to coat the vegetables evenly. Lightly season with salt and pepper.
3. Spread the vegetables on one-half of the baking sheet.
4. Lightly season the chicken breasts with salt and pepper.
5. In a large skillet, heat the remaining 1 tablespoon of oil over medium-high heat and brown the chicken on both sides, about 4 minutes total.
6. Place the chicken on the other half of the baking sheet, spread evenly with the sauce, and top with the cheese.
7. Bake until the chicken is just cooked through and the vegetables are tender, 25 to 30 minutes.

REHEATING TIP: To reheat, microwave uncovered for 30-second intervals until heated through. To reheat from frozen, thaw in the refrigerator overnight before reheating as directed.

Per serving: Calories: 425; Total fat: 17g; Saturated fat: 5g; Protein: 35g; Total carbs: 35g; Fiber: 10g; Sugar: 13g; Sodium: 291mg

GLUTEN-FREE • NUT-FREE • VEGETARIAN

PUMPKIN PIE TOFU "MILKSHAKE"

SERVINGS: 5 • **PREP TIME:** 10 minutes, plus 2 hours to freeze

Pumpkin is an exciting and delicious ingredient, wonderful for both sweet and savory recipes. This creamy, thick smoothie uses canned unsweetened pumpkin because it is readily available and inexpensive. To elevate the taste even further, you can use fresh pumpkin cut into 1-inch cubes and roasted in a 400°F oven until lightly caramelized and tender.

- 1 (28-ounce) can pumpkin puree
- 14 ounces extra-firm tofu, cut into ½-inch cubes
- 5 cups 2 percent milk or unsweetened almond milk
- 10 tablespoons maple syrup
- 1¼ teaspoons pumpkin pie spice

1. Scoop the pumpkin puree into 2 ice cube trays and place the trays in the freezer to freeze solid, about 2 hours.
2. Spread out the tofu on a small baking sheet and place in the freezer until frozen, about 1 hour.
3. Evenly divide the milk, maple syrup, and pumpkin pie spice among 5 medium containers with tight seals.
4. Divide the frozen pumpkin and tofu cubes among 5 medium sealable bags (3 bags will have an extra pumpkin cube).
5. Take one bag of pumpkin and tofu out of the freezer and place the cubes in a blender along with 1 container of the milk and syrup mixture and pulse until smooth. Serve immediately.

SUBSTITUTION TIP: If you are not a fan of tofu, use plain Greek yogurt instead to create a thick, creamy texture. Add the yogurt to the milk and syrup mixture.

Per serving: Calories: 338; Total fat: 8g; Saturated fat: 2g; Protein: 18g; Total carbs: 55g; Fiber: 5g; Sugar: 42g; Sodium: 127mg

CHAPTER 8

Week 8 Prep

Crêpes with Raspberries 85

Spinach Mac and Cheese 86

Simple Slow Cooker Chicken Stew 87

Cashew-Crusted Halibut with Brown Rice 88

Classic Hummus 89

Week 8 includes some international flair with French crêpes and Middle Eastern hummus, along with comforting mac and cheese and a filling stew. Golden cashew-crusted fish rounds out an exciting menu. If you do not have a slow cooker, you can certainly use a stockpot for the stew instead if you brown the chicken, onion, and garlic before adding everything else. The recipe for hummus calls for pita chips, but you can serve it with flatbread or a handful of carrot sticks. The choice is yours!

Crêpes with Raspberries, page 85

SHOPPING LIST

5-INGREDIENT PANTRY

- *Black pepper, freshly ground*
- *Garlic, minced (2 teaspoons)*
- *Nonstick cooking spray*
- *Oil, olive (3 tablespoons)*
- *Onion, sweet (1)*
- *Salt, sea*

MEAT, POULTRY, OR SEAFOOD

- Chicken, boneless, skinless breasts (1 pound)
- Halibut, 3 (5-ounce) boneless fillets

DAIRY AND NONDAIRY SUBSTITUTES

- Butter (3 tablespoons)
- Cheddar cheese, aged, shredded (1 cup)
- Eggs, large (2)
- Milk, 2 percent (1 cup)

PRODUCE

- Baby spinach (2 cups)
- Carrots (3)
- Celery (2 stalks)
- Garlic (3 cloves)
- Green beans (8 ounces)
- Lemon (1)
- Potatoes, russet (2)
- Raspberries (5 cups)

CANNED AND JARRED

- Chickpeas, low-sodium (1 [15-ounce] can)
- Evaporated milk (1 cup)
- Tahini (½ cup)

PANTRY

- Cashews, chopped (½ cup)
- Chicken broth, low-sodium (2 cups)
- Flour, all-purpose (1¼ cups)
- Macaroni, whole-wheat (6 ounces)
- Nutmeg, ground (⅛ teaspoon)
- Rice, brown (¾ cup)

OTHER

- Bread crumbs, seasoned (½ cup)
- Pita chips (5 ounces)

	BREAKFAST	LUNCH	DINNER	SNACK/DESSERT
DAY 1	Crêpes with Raspberries	Spinach Mac and Cheese	Cashew-Crusted Halibut with Brown Rice	Classic Hummus
DAY 2	Crêpes with Raspberries	Simple Slow Cooker Chicken Stew	Cashew-Crusted Halibut with Brown Rice	Classic Hummus
DAY 3	Crêpes with Raspberries	Simple Slow Cooker Chicken Stew	Cashew-Crusted Halibut with Brown Rice	Classic Hummus
DAY 4	Crêpes with Raspberries	Spinach Mac and Cheese	Simple Slow Cooker Chicken Stew	Classic Hummus
DAY 5	Crêpes with Raspberries	Spinach Mac and Cheese	Simple Slow Cooker Chicken Stew	Classic Hummus

STEP-BY-STEP PREP

1. Prepare the vegetables needed for all the recipes:
   - Peel the carrots and cut into rounds.
   - Peel the russet potatoes and dice.
   - Chop the onion.
   - Dice the celery stalks.
   - Trim the green beans.
2. Cube the chicken breast for the Simple Slow Cooker Chicken Stew (page 87).
3. Combine all the ingredients as directed for the chicken stew and start the slow cooker.
4. Preheat the oven to 350°F.

5. Cook the pasta according to the package directions and cook the spinach for the Spinach Mac and Cheese (page 86).

6. Make the Classic Hummus (page 89) recipe completely. Evenly divide the hummus among 5 small containers, cover, label, and store in the refrigerator for up to 1 week. Divide the pita chips among 5 small sealable plastic bags, label, and store at room temperature for up to 1 week.

7. When the pasta and spinach are cooked, put together the complete mac and cheese recipe and place the casserole in the oven to bake.

8. Cook the rice for the Cashew-Crusted Halibut with Brown Rice (page 88).

9. Prepare the Crêpes with Raspberries (page 85) recipe completely and place 2 crêpes in one section of each of 5 large (2-compartment) meal prep containers and 1 cup of raspberries in the other side of each. Cover, label, and store in the refrigerator for up to 5 days.

10. When the Spinach Mac and Cheese is finished, transfer to 3 large meal prep containers. Cover, label, and store 1 container in the refrigerator for up to 3 days and 2 in the freezer for up to 1 month.

11. Increase the oven temperature to 400°F.

12. Prepare the fish and green beans for the halibut recipe and place the baking sheet in the oven.

13. When the fish and beans are done, place one fish fillet in 1 compartment of 3 large (3-compartment) containers and evenly divide the roasted green beans among the containers. Fill the last empty compartment with the cooked rice, about ½ cup in each. Place the containers uncovered in the refrigerator to cool completely. When cool, cover, label, and store the meals in the refrigerator for up to 5 days.

14. Transfer the chicken stew from the slow cooker to 4 large meal prep containers and place them in the refrigerator to cool. When the stew is cool, seal, label, and store 2 of the containers in the refrigerator for up to 3 days and 2 in the freezer for up to 1 month.

NUT-FREE • **VEGETARIAN**

CRÊPES with RASPBERRIES

SERVINGS: 5 • **PREP TIME:** 10 minutes • **COOK TIME:** 25 minutes

Crêpes are thought to have originated in Brittany, France, in the 12th century using buckwheat flour because this grain grew well in the wet agricultural conditions. This version is made with all-purpose flour instead, so the finished crêpes are delicate and a light golden brown. If you enjoy a savory version, place a thin slice of ham and a scattering of cheese in the middle of the cooled crêpe before folding it up.

1 cup 2 percent milk, at room temperature

⅓ cup water, at room temperature

3 tablespoons melted butter

2 large eggs, at room temperature

¼ teaspoon sea salt

1¼ cups all-purpose flour

Nonstick cooking spray

5 cups raspberries

1. In a large bowl, whisk together milk, water, melted butter, eggs, and salt until well blended.

2. Whisk in the flour until very smooth. Transfer the batter to a large liquid measuring cup or pitcher.

3. Place a medium nonstick skillet or crêpe pan over medium-high heat and spray it with cooking spray. Pour the batter into the skillet, about ¼ cup for each crêpe. Tilt the skillet so that the batter coats the surface evenly and thinly.

4. Cook the crêpe for about 2 minutes, then loosen it, flip it over, and cook the other side for about 30 seconds.

5. Remove the crêpe from the skillet and place it on a parchment-covered plate.

6. Repeat with the remaining batter to create 10 crêpes. Let the crêpes cool and fold each into quarters. Divide the raspberries equally among each serving and wash the berries just before eating.

REHEATING TIP: Wrap the crêpes in a paper towel and microwave for 30-second intervals until heated through.

Per serving: Calories: 297; Total fat: 11g; Saturated fat: 6g; Protein: 9g; Total carbs: 41g; Fiber: 9g; Sugar: 8g; Sodium: 222mg

NUT-FREE • VEGETARIAN

SPINACH MAC and CHEESE

SERVINGS: 3 • **PREP TIME:** 5 minutes • **COOK TIME:** 40 minutes

Mac and cheese is the ultimate comfort food—filling, cheesy, and creamy. The use of whole-wheat pasta adds some healthy fiber, and evaporated milk is lower in calories and fat compared to heavier cream versions of the sauce.

2 teaspoons olive oil, divided

6 ounces whole-wheat elbow macaroni

2 cups fresh baby spinach

1 cup evaporated milk

1 cup shredded aged cheddar cheese

Sea salt

Freshly ground black pepper

½ cup seasoned bread crumbs

1. Preheat the oven to 350°F. Lightly grease a 9-by-9-inch casserole dish with 1 teaspoon of olive oil and set aside.

2. Place a medium saucepan filled with water on high heat and bring to a boil. Cook the macaroni until al dente according to the package directions. Remove from heat, stir the spinach into the macaroni and hot water, and let stand for 3 minutes. Drain and rinse in cool water. Transfer to the baking dish.

3. In a large saucepan over medium heat, bring the evaporated milk to a simmer.

4. Whisk in the cheese until melted, about 2 minutes. Add the cheese sauce to the macaroni and stir until well mixed. Season with salt and pepper.

5. In a small bowl, stir together the bread crumbs and the remaining 1 teaspoon of olive oil. Top the casserole with the bread crumb mixture.

6. Bake until bubbly and lightly browned, about 20 minutes.

REHEATING TIP: To reheat, microwave uncovered for 30-second intervals until heated through. To reheat from frozen, thaw in the refrigerator overnight before reheating as directed.

INGREDIENT TIP: The flavor of the dish is completely dependent on the quality and flavor of the cheese. Aged cheddar has a lovely sharp taste, but Gruyère or Swiss will add a smoky flavor. Try different cheeses to suit your taste.

Per serving: Calories: 506; Total fat: 16g; Saturated fat: 8g; Protein: 27g; Total carbs: 66g; Fiber: 6g; Sugar: 11g; Sodium: 393mg

DAIRY-FREE • GLUTEN-FREE • NUT-FREE

SIMPLE SLOW COOKER CHICKEN STEW

SERVINGS: 4 • **PREP TIME:** 15 minutes • **COOK TIME:** 3 to 4 hours

Slow cooker meals are a cornerstone of meal prep because they allow you to create an entire recipe without having to supervise it, so you can concentrate on the other recipes on your cook day. This dish is packed with tender chunks of chicken and vegetables in a flavorful broth. If you enjoy a thicker stew, combine 1 tablespoon of cornstarch with ¼ cup of water and stir it into the finished stew before shutting off the slow cooker.

Nonstick cooking spray

3 carrots, cut into rounds

2 russet potatoes, diced into ½-inch chunks

1 sweet onion, chopped

2 celery stalks, diced

2 teaspoons minced garlic

1 pound boneless, skinless chicken breast, cut into 1-inch cubes

2 cups low-sodium chicken broth

Sea salt

Freshly ground black pepper

1. Grease the insert of the slow cooker with cooking spray.
2. Add the carrots, potatoes, onion, celery, and garlic and stir to combine.
3. Place the chicken on top of the vegetables and pour in the broth. Season lightly with salt and pepper.
4. Cover and cook on high for 3 to 4 hours.

REHEATING TIP: To reheat, microwave uncovered for 30-second intervals until heated through. To reheat from frozen, thaw in the refrigerator overnight before reheating as directed.

Per serving: Calories: 356; Total fat: 5g; Saturated fat: 1g; Protein: 43g; Total carbs: 32g; Fiber: 4g; Sugar: 7g; Sodium: 163mg

DAIRY-FREE • GLUTEN-FREE

CASHEW-CRUSTED HALIBUT with BROWN RICE

SERVINGS: 3 • **PREP TIME:** 15 minutes • **COOK TIME:** 35 minutes

Halibut is a beautiful fish; it is firm, slightly sweet, and moist. It's often used for fish and chips because it cooks quickly, so you don't end up with finished batter and raw fish. The speedy cooking time is also ideal for sheet-pan recipes and meal prep. Try a scoop of homemade or store-bought tartar sauce or a squeeze of lemon to perk up the flavors.

¾ cup brown rice

1½ cups water

3 (5-ounce) boneless halibut fillets

Sea salt

½ cup finely chopped cashews

Nonstick cooking spray

8 ounces green beans, trimmed

1 teaspoon olive oil

⅛ teaspoon ground nutmeg

Freshly ground black pepper

1. Preheat the oven to 400°F. Line a baking sheet with parchment paper.

2. Add the rice and 1¼ cups water to a large saucepan over high heat. Bring to a boil, cover, reduce the heat to low, and simmer 35 minutes. Remove the rice from the heat and let stand covered for 10 minutes. Fluff with a fork.

3. While the rice is cooking, pat the fish dry with paper towels and season it lightly with salt.

4. Place the chopped cashews in a small bowl and dredge the fish fillets in the nuts to coat both sides evenly.

5. Grease the baking sheet lightly with cooking spray and place the fish on one half.

6. In a medium bowl, toss the green beans with the oil and nutmeg. Spread the beans on the other half of the baking sheet and lightly season with salt and pepper.

7. Bake the fish and beans until the fish is golden and flakes easily with a fork, about 15 minutes.

REHEATING TIP: To reheat, microwave uncovered for 30-second intervals until heated through.

Per serving: Calories: 514; Total fat: 18g; Saturated fat: 4g; Protein: 40g; Total carbs: 49g; Fiber: 4g; Sugar: 4g; Sodium: 80mg

DAIRY-FREE • GLUTEN-FREE • NUT-FREE • VEGAN

CLASSIC HUMMUS

SERVINGS: 5 • **PREP TIME:** 10 minutes

Hummus is one of those all-purpose creations that can be used on sandwiches, as a dip for vegetables, as a topping for fish or chicken, and in sauces and soups for extra flavor. So double the recipe if you want to use it in other dishes or with other meal prep menus. Hummus can be made with almost any type of legume such as cannellini beans, lentils, navy beans, or even black beans.

1 (15-ounce) can low-sodium chickpeas, drained and rinsed, 2 to 3 tablespoons liquid reserved

½ cup tahini

3 garlic cloves

Juice of 1 lemon

2 tablespoons olive oil

Sea salt

Pita chips, for serving

1. Put the chickpeas, tahini, garlic, lemon juice, and olive oil in a food processor or blender and pulse until blended but not entirely smooth. If it's too thick, add 1 tablespoon of reserved liquid at a time until the desired consistency is reached.

2. Season with salt and serve with pita chips.

Per serving: Calories: 404; Total fat: 24g; Saturated fat: 3g; Protein: 12g; Total carbs: 38g; Fiber: 7g; Sugar: 4g; Sodium: 219mg

CHAPTER 9

Week 9 Prep

Granola Muesli 95

Sheet-Pan Sausage and Peppers 96

Baked Lemon Garlic Trout with Potato Wedges 97

Creamy Curry Chicken and Rice 98

Crispy Chili Kale Chips 99

This week highlights assertive flavors inspired by Thailand and India, as well as a classic Canadian fish preparation. The prep this week is one of the quickest, but you will need two baking sheets to get everything done. If you don't have two, you can adjust the step-by-step plan to stagger the kale chips to bake in batches and the granola and trout recipes to bake one after the other.

Sheet-Pan Sausage and Peppers, page 96

SHOPPING LIST

5-INGREDIENT PANTRY

- *Garlic, minced (1 tablespoon)*
- *Nonstick cooking spray*
- *Oil, olive (5 tablespoons)*
- *Onion, sweet (2)*
- *Salt, sea*

MEAT, POULTRY, OR SEAFOOD

- Chicken, boneless, skinless breasts (1 pound)
- Sausages, Italian, sweet (1 pound)
- Trout, 3 (5-ounce) boneless, skinless fillets

DAIRY AND NONDAIRY SUBSTITUTES

- Milk, 2 percent (2 cups)
- Yogurt, Greek, vanilla (1¼ cups)

PRODUCE

- Bell peppers (4)
- Blueberries (2½ cups)
- Kale (5 cups)
- Lemon (1)
- Potatoes, russet (3)

CANNED AND JARRED

- Coconut milk, full fat (1 [15-ounce] can)
- Tomatoes, diced, low-sodium (1 [28-ounce] can)

PANTRY

- Chicken broth, low-sodium (2 cups)
- Chili powder (½ teaspoon)
- Cumin, ground (¼ teaspoon)
- Curry powder (2 tablespoons)
- Farro (1 cup)
- Granola (2½ cups)
- Paprika, smoked (¼ teaspoon)
- Rice, white (1 cup)
- Sunflower seeds, roasted, unsalted (¾ cup)

	BREAKFAST	LUNCH	DINNER	SNACK/DESSERT
DAY 1	Granola Muesli	Sheet-Pan Sausage and Peppers	Baked Lemon Garlic Trout with Potato Wedges	Crispy Chili Kale Chips
DAY 2	Granola Muesli	Creamy Curry Chicken and Rice	Baked Lemon Garlic Trout with Potato Wedges	Crispy Chili Kale Chips
DAY 3	Granola Muesli	Creamy Curry Chicken and Rice	Baked Lemon Garlic Trout with Potato Wedges	Crispy Chili Kale Chips
DAY 4	Granola Muesli	Sheet-Pan Sausage and Peppers	Creamy Curry Chicken and Rice	Crispy Chili Kale Chips
DAY 5	Granola Muesli	Sheet-Pan Sausage and Peppers	Creamy Curry Chicken and Rice	Crispy Chili Kale Chips

STEP-BY-STEP PREP

1. Preheat the oven to 300°F.
2. Cube the chicken for the Creamy Curry Chicken and Rice (page 98). Place all the ingredients for the recipe in the slow cooker and start it.
3. Make the Crispy Chili Kale Chips (page 99) and place them in the oven to roast.
4. Make the Granola Muesli (page 95) completely. Seal, label, and store in the refrigerator for up to 5 days.
5. Remove the kale chips from the oven and transfer them to a rack to cool.
6. Increase the oven temperature to 375°F.

7. Prepare the potatoes for the Baked Lemon Garlic Trout with Potato Wedges (page 97) and place them in the oven to roast.

8. Place the sausages for the Sheet-Pan Sausages and Peppers (page 96) on one-third of another baking sheet, pricking them all over with a fork.

9. Prepare the vegetables for the sausage dish and spread them on the empty two-thirds of the baking sheet. When the potato wedges are finished in the oven, bake the sausage and vegetables for 35 minutes.

10. Cook the farro for the sausage and peppers. Remove the sausage and vegetables from the oven when finished.

11. Add the fish to the baking sheet with the potato wedges and place back in the oven to roast.

12. Cook the rice for the curry.

13. Divide the cooled kale chips among 5 medium meal prep containers and store them at room temperature for up to 5 days.

14. When the rice is finished, evenly divide it among 4 large (2-compartment) containers, placing about ½ cup in the smaller section of each. Place the containers in the refrigerator to cool.

15. Place one fish fillet on one side of 3 large (2-compartment) meal prep containers and evenly divide the potatoes into the other side of the containers. Seal, label, and store in the refrigerator for up to 3 days.

16. Place the sausage and peppers on one side of 4 large (2-compartment) meal prep containers and evenly divide the farro into the other side of the containers. Seal, label, and store 2 in the refrigerator for up to 3 days and 2 in the freezer for up to 1 month.

17. When the curry is ready, divide it among the containers with the rice. Store 2 in the refrigerator for up to 5 days and 2 in the freezer for up to 1 month.

GLUTEN-FREE • VEGETARIAN

GRANOLA MUESLI

SERVINGS: 5 • **PREP TIME:** 10 minutes

To make this muesli, look for granola with a nice mix of nuts, dried fruit, oats, and coconut for optimum taste and texture. Any extra granola can be used as a topping on other meal prep recipes such as parfaits, pancakes, and muffins. You can also eat a handful by itself for an energy-packed snack.

2½ cups granola, store-bought or homemade Quinoa Pecan Granola (page 137)

¾ cup roasted unsalted sunflower seeds (optional)

2 cups 2 percent milk

1¼ cup vanilla Greek yogurt

2½ cups fresh blueberries

1. In a medium bowl, mix together the granola and sunflower seeds (if using) until combined.
2. Evenly divide the granola mixture into 5 medium meal prep containers. Evenly distribute the milk and yogurt among the containers and stir to combine well. Top with blueberries.

Per serving: Calories: 209; Total fat: 6g; Saturated fat: 3g; Protein: 7g; Total carbs: 33g; Fiber: 4g; Sugar: 19g; Sodium: 174mg

DAIRY-FREE • GLUTEN-FREE • NUT-FREE

SHEET-PAN SAUSAGE *and* PEPPERS

SERVINGS: 4 • **PREP TIME:** 15 minutes • **COOK TIME:** 35 minutes

Sausage and peppers is a classic Italian American dish, brought to North American shores by Italian immigrants. Peppers are an excellent source of calcium, potassium, and vitamins A, B, C, and E. Add farro for a nutritious meal that can help prevent cardiovascular disease and boost your immune system.

1 pound sweet Italian sausage

4 bell peppers, mixed colors, seeded and cut into ½-inch slices

1 sweet onion, halved and cut into ½-inch slices

2 teaspoons olive oil

Sea salt

1 cup farro, rinsed

2 cups low-sodium chicken broth

1. Preheat the oven to 375°F. Line a baking sheet with parchment paper.

2. Place the sausage on one-third of the sheet and prick them all over with a fork.

3. In a large bowl, toss the peppers and onion with the oil until the vegetables are well coated, then transfer them to the empty two-thirds of the baking sheet. Season the vegetables with salt.

4. Bake until the sausage is no longer pink and the vegetables are tender, turning all the ingredients halfway through, about 35 minutes total.

5. While the sausage and peppers are cooking, combine the farro and chicken broth in a medium saucepan over medium-high heat. Bring to a boil, then reduce the heat to low and simmer until the broth is absorbed, about 20 minutes.

6. Remove the sausage and peppers from the oven and let the sausage cool enough to handle it, about 15 minutes. Cut the sausage into ½-inch rounds and add it back to the pepper mixture, tossing to combine.

REHEATING TIP: To reheat, microwave uncovered for 30-second intervals until heated through. To reheat from frozen, thaw in the refrigerator overnight before reheating as directed.

Per serving: Calories: 422; Total fat: 15g; Saturated fat: 4g; Protein: 27g; Total carbs: 48g; Fiber: 5g; Sugar: 4g; Sodium: 498mg

DAIRY-FREE • GLUTEN-FREE • NUT-FREE

BAKED LEMON GARLIC TROUT *with* POTATO WEDGES

SERVINGS: 3 • **PREP TIME:** 15 minutes • **COOK TIME:** 50 minutes

Trout is best prepared as a shore lunch—freshly caught, cleaned, and cooked in a huge, ancient skillet along with potatoes and lots of garlic and onion. You will be using an oven and a baking sheet instead of a campfire and cast-iron pan, but the taste of this meal will be almost identical, just not as smoky. If you can't get trout, try tilapia, catfish, or haddock, fresh or flash-frozen and thawed overnight in the refrigerator.

3 large russet potatoes, cuts into eighths

3 tablespoons olive oil, divided

¼ teaspoon smoked paprika

Sea salt

3 (5-ounce) boneless, skinless trout fillets

Freshly ground black pepper

1 teaspoon minced garlic

1 lemon, thinly cut into at least 9 slices

1. Preheat the oven to 375°F. Line a baking sheet with parchment paper.
2. In a large bowl, toss together the potatoes, 2 tablespoons of oil, and the paprika. Spread the potatoes on one-half of the baking sheet and season lightly with salt.
3. Bake the potatoes for 30 minutes, then remove from the oven and place the trout on the other half of the baking sheet. Brush the trout with the remaining 1 tablespoon of olive oil, season with salt and pepper, spread with the garlic and arrange the lemon slices on top.
4. Place the baking sheet back in the oven and bake until the potatoes are golden and lightly crispy and the fish is cooked through, about 20 minutes.

REHEATING TIP: To reheat, microwave uncovered for 30-second intervals until heated through.

Per serving: Calories: 458; Total fat: 18g; Saturated fat: 3g; Protein: 33g; Total carbs: 39g; Fiber: 3g; Sugar: 1g; Sodium: 55mg

DAIRY-FREE • GLUTEN-FREE • NUT-FREE

CREAMY CURRY CHICKEN and RICE

SERVINGS: 4 • **PREP TIME:** 15 minutes • **COOK TIME:** 3 to 4 hours

Curry is a never-fail dish, made easier with the many fabulous spice blends available in the grocery store. You can find complete packages of pastes, dried herbs, and even garnishes to create curry dishes from all over the world. The recommendation in this dish is two tablespoons of a spice mix, but you can add whatever amount or type you prefer.

Nonstick cooking spray

1 (28-ounce) can low-sodium diced tomatoes

1 (15-ounce) can full-fat coconut milk

1 sweet onion, chopped

2 teaspoons minced garlic

2 tablespoons curry powder, mild or hot

1 pound boneless, skinless chicken breasts, cut into 1-inch cubes

1 cup white rice

2 cups water

1. Lightly grease the slow cooker insert with cooking spray.

2. Place the tomatoes, coconut milk, onion, garlic, and curry powder in the slow cooker and stir together until well mixed. Add the chicken.

3. Cover and cook on high for 3 to 4 hours.

4. While the curry is cooking, stir together the rice and water in a medium saucepan over medium-high heat and bring to a boil. Reduce the heat to low, cover, and simmer until the liquid is absorbed, about 20 minutes.

REHEATING TIP: To reheat, microwave uncovered for 30-second intervals until heated through. To reheat from frozen, thaw in the refrigerator overnight before reheating as directed.

Per serving: Calories: 593; Total fat: 27g; Saturated fat: 19g; Protein: 33g; Total carbs: 57g; Fiber: 7g; Sugar: 10g; Sodium: 95mg

DAIRY-FREE • GLUTEN-FREE • NUT-FREE • VEGAN

CRISPY CHILI KALE CHIPS

SERVINGS: 5 • **PREP TIME:** 15 minutes • **COOK TIME:** 25 minutes

Kale chips are available premade in most stores, but they can be expensive considering they are a very simple snack. So it's lucky you can make your own so easily for the cost of a bunch of fresh kale! Kale chips are best eaten in the first few days but can be stored at room temperature for the full 5 days of this meal plan (they just might not be as crispy on the last day).

5 cups fresh kale, stemmed and torn into 2-inch pieces

1 tablespoon olive oil

½ teaspoon chili powder

¼ teaspoon ground cumin

¼ teaspoon sea salt

1. Preheat the oven to 300°F. Line 2 baking sheets with parchment paper.
2. Dry the kale completely and transfer to a large bowl.
3. Add the olive oil to the bowl and toss to evenly coat each leaf.
4. Season with chili, cumin, and salt and toss to coat.
5. Evenly divide the kale between the baking sheets, spreading in a single layer.
6. Bake the kale, flipping halfway through, until the kale is crispy and dry, about 25 minutes.
7. Transfer the kale chips to a rack and cool completely.

SUBSTITUTION TIP: Kale chips can be seasoned with an assortment of herbs and spices. Try coriander, curry, nutmeg, or blends such as garam masala or ras el hanout for different flavors.

Per serving: Calories: 33; Total fat: 3g; Saturated fat: 0g; Protein: 1g; Total carbs: 2g; Fiber: 1g; Sugar: 0g; Sodium: 131mg

CHAPTER 10

Week 10 Prep

Sweet Potato Spinach Frittata 105

Salad Bowls with Tzatziki Sauce 106

Korean-Style Beef with Brown Rice 107

Paprika Chicken with Butter Noodles 108

Roasted Red Pepper Spread 109

You will be enjoying lots of vegetables this week alongside an assortment of proteins including eggs, chicken, and ground beef with Asian-inspired flavors. A simple salad bowl and a blender-prepared dip cut down on prep time without sacrificing any flavor. You will be using a store-bought rotisserie chicken in the menu, and you can certainly package up the remaining meat for another week. However, in the interest of no waste, you can throw the extra shredded chicken into the frittata for a protein-powered breakfast.

Roasted Red Pepper Spread, page 109

SHOPPING LIST

5-INGREDIENT PANTRY

- *Black pepper, freshly ground*
- *Garlic, minced (4½ teaspoons)*
- *Oil, olive (¼ cup)*
- *Onion, sweet (2)*
- *Salt, sea*

MEAT, POULTRY, OR SEAFOOD

- Beef, ground, extra-lean (1 pound)
- Chicken, 3 (5-ounce) boneless, skinless breasts
- Chicken, rotisserie (1)

DAIRY AND NONDAIRY SUBSTITUTES

- Butter (3 tablespoons)
- Eggs, large (10)
- Goat cheese (2 ounces)
- Milk, 2 percent (¼ cup)
- Tzatziki sauce (¾ cup)

PRODUCE

- Baby spinach (2 cups)
- Bell peppers, red (2)
- Bok choy, baby (2 cups shredded, about 6 baby bok choy)
- Cucumbers, English (2)
- Lemon (1)
- Parsley, fresh (1 bunch)
- Sweet potatoes (2)
- Tomatoes, cherry (2 cups)

CANNED AND JARRED

- Barbecue sauce, Korean beef (¾ cup)
- Chickpeas, low-sodium (1 [15-ounce] can)
- Peppers, red, roasted (2 [6-ounce] jars)

PANTRY

- Cumin, ground (1 teaspoon)
- Egg noodles, wide (6 ounces)
- Paprika, smoked (½ teaspoon)
- Pecans, chopped (½ cup)
- Rice, brown (1 cup)

OTHER

- Pita chips (5 ounces)

	BREAKFAST	LUNCH	DINNER	SNACK/DESSERT
DAY 1	Sweet Potato Spinach Frittata	Salad Bowls with Tzatziki Sauce	Korean-Style Beef with Brown Rice	Roasted Red Pepper Spread
DAY 2	Sweet Potato Spinach Frittata	Salad Bowls with Tzatziki Sauce	Paprika Chicken with Butter Noodles	Roasted Red Pepper Spread
DAY 3	Sweet Potato Spinach Frittata	Salad Bowls with Tzatziki Sauce	Korean-Style Beef with Brown Rice	Roasted Red Pepper Spread
DAY 4	Sweet Potato Spinach Frittata	Paprika Chicken with Butter Noodles	Korean-Style Beef with Brown Rice	Roasted Red Pepper Spread
DAY 5	Sweet Potato Spinach Frittata	Korean-Style Beef with Brown Rice	Paprika Chicken with Butter Noodles	Roasted Red Pepper Spread

STEP-BY-STEP PREP

THE NIGHT BEFORE YOUR COOKING DAY

1. Place 1 cup of brown rice and 3 cups of water in a medium container, seal, and soak overnight in the refrigerator.

ON YOUR COOKING DAY

1. Preheat the oven to broil.

2. Cook the rice for the Korean-Style Beef with Brown Rice (page 107).

3. Prepare the Sweet Potato Spinach Frittata (page 105) recipe completely and set aside to cool.

4. Transfer the cooked rice to 4 large meal prep containers and set aside.

5. Make the Roasted Red Pepper Spread (page 109) recipe completely and evenly divide the dip among 5 medium meal prep containers. Seal, label, and store in the refrigerator for up to 5 days. Place the chips in 5 small sealable plastic bags, label, and store at room temperature for up to 1 week.

6. Divide the frittata into 5 portions and store in 5 large meal prep containers. Seal, label, and store 3 of the containers in the refrigerator for up to 3 days and 2 of the containers in the freezer for up to 1 month.

7. Make the beef and vegetables for the Korean-style beef and transfer the mixture to the containers with the rice. Seal, label, and store 2 of the containers in the refrigerator for up to 3 days and 2 of the containers in the freezer for up to 1 month.

8. Preheat the oven to 350°F.

9. Prepare the chicken for the Paprika Chicken with Butter Noodles (page 108) recipe and place in the oven to roast.

10. Make the Salad Bowls with Tzatziki Sauce recipe (page 106) completely. Seal, label, and store the salad and the sauce containers in the refrigerator for up to 5 days.

11. Take the chicken out of the oven and let sit for 10 minutes. Cook the noodles for the recipe while the chicken is resting.

12. Cut each chicken breast on a bias into 3 pieces and place each breast in 1 compartment of 3 large (2-compartment) containers. Evenly divide the noodles into the empty compartment of the containers and put the containers in the refrigerator to cool.

13. When cool, cover, label, and store 1 container in the refrigerator for up to 3 days and 2 containers in the freezer for up to 1 month.

GLUTEN-FREE • NUT-FREE • VEGETARIAN

SWEET POTATO SPINACH FRITTATA

SERVINGS: 5 • **PREP TIME:** 10 minutes • **COOK TIME:** 26 minutes

Frittatas are often confused with omelets and quiches because they contain many of the same ingredients. The cooking techniques are different, though. Frittatas are meant to be broiled at the end of the process to create the signature puffy golden top, which also melts the cheese topping. Serve with fresh fruit for a sweet counterpart and a pretty presentation.

1 tablespoon olive oil

2 sweet potatoes, diced into ¼-inch cubes

1 sweet onion, chopped

1 teaspoon minced garlic

2 cups fresh baby spinach

10 large eggs

¼ cup 2 percent milk

Sea salt

Freshly ground black pepper

½ cup crumbled goat cheese

1. Preheat the oven to broil.
2. In a large oven-proof skillet, heat the oil over medium-high heat.
3. Add the sweet potatoes and sauté until cooked through and lightly browned, about 10 minutes.
4. Add the onion and garlic and sauté for 3 minutes more.
5. Add the spinach and sauté until wilted, about 3 minutes.
6. In a medium bowl, whisk together the eggs and milk. Season lightly with salt and pepper.
7. Pour the egg mixture into the skillet and cook, lifting the edges to let the uncooked egg flow under the cooked portions, until the bottom is set and the top almost cooked through, about 8 minutes.
8. Sprinkle the top with the cheese and place the skillet in the oven. Broil until the top is puffy and golden, about 2 minutes.
9. Let the frittata cool for about 15 minutes, then cut into 5 portions.

REHEATING TIP: Eat this meal cold or reheat by microwaving uncovered for 30-second intervals until heated through. To reheat from frozen, thaw in the refrigerator overnight before reheating as directed.

Per serving: Calories: 271; Total fat: 15g; Saturated fat: 5g; Protein: 17g; Total carbs: 17g; Fiber: 2g; Sugar: 7g; Sodium: 243mg

GLUTEN-FREE • NUT-FREE

SALAD BOWLS with TZATZIKI SAUCE

SERVINGS: 3 • **PREP TIME:** 15 minutes

This simple dish has wonderfully complex flavors. Fresh vegetables, tender chicken, and buttery chickpeas are enhanced by the addition of a fresh, tart yogurt-based sauce. If you want to include greens, add 2 cups of chopped fresh romaine to the dish, piling it right on top of the other ingredients in the meal prep container.

1 (15-ounce) can low-sodium chickpeas, drained and rinsed

3 cups cooked, shredded rotisserie chicken

2 English cucumbers, diced

2 cups halved cherry tomatoes

¾ cup store-bought tzatziki sauce or homemade Tzatziki Sauce (page 178)

1. Divide the chickpeas among 3 large meal prep containers. Top with the chicken, cucumber, and tomatoes and seal the containers.

2. Evenly divide the tzatziki sauce among 3 (2-ounce) containers.

Per serving: Calories: 414; Total fat: 14g; Saturated fat: 4g; Protein: 45g; Total carbs: 27g; Fiber: 8g; Sugar: 11g; Sodium: 217mg

DAIRY-FREE • GLUTEN-FREE • NUT-FREE

KOREAN-STYLE BEEF with BROWN RICE

SERVINGS: 4 • **PREP TIME:** 15 minutes • **COOK TIME:** 25 minutes

Korean-style beef is often made with thinly sliced sirloin rather than the budget-friendly ground beef used in this dish. The benefit beyond the cost savings is that ground beef soaks up the sauce very well, creating an extra-flavorful result. The added vegetables keep the dish from being too rich and contain fiber and healthy antioxidants.

1 cup brown rice, soaked overnight in 3 cups water

2 cups water

1 pound extra-lean ground beef

1 sweet onion, chopped

2 teaspoons minced garlic

2 cups shredded baby bok choy

2 red bell peppers, seeded and thinly sliced

¾ cup store-bought Korean-style beef barbecue sauce

1. Drain the rice and combine it with the 2 cups of water in a large saucepan over high heat. Bring to a boil, cover, then reduce the heat to low and simmer until the liquid is absorbed, about 25 minutes.

2. While the rice is cooking, brown the beef in a large skillet over medium-high heat until cooked through, 7 to 8 minutes. Stir in the onion and garlic and sauté for 3 minutes longer.

3. Add the bok choy and peppers and sauté for 6 minutes.

4. Add the barbecue sauce and sauté until heated through, about 5 minutes.

REHEATING TIP: To reheat, microwave uncovered for 30-second intervals until heated through. To reheat from frozen, thaw in the refrigerator overnight before reheating as directed.

Per serving: Calories: 427; Total fat: 7g; Saturated fat: 3g; Protein: 32g; Total carbs: 57g; Fiber: 5g; Sugar: 16g; Sodium: 621mg

NUT-FREE

PAPRIKA CHICKEN *with* BUTTER NOODLES

SERVINGS: 3 • **PREP TIME:** 5 minutes • **COOK TIME:** 20 minutes

This dish is a simplified chicken paprikash, without the high calories and fat-laden sauce. Paprika is a ground spice made from dried sweet peppers or, in the case of this recipe with smoked paprika, smoked and dried peppers. This popular, brightly hued spice is a staple in Hungarian and Spanish cuisine, adding color and delightful flavor to many traditional dishes.

1 tablespoon olive oil

3 (5-ounce) boneless, skinless chicken breasts

½ teaspoon smoked paprika

Sea salt

6 ounces wide egg noodles

3 tablespoons butter

1 tablespoon chopped fresh parsley

Freshly ground black pepper

1. Preheat the oven to 350°F. Line a 9-inch square baking dish with parchment paper.
2. In a large skillet, heat the oil over medium-high heat.
3. Sprinkle the chicken breasts all over with the paprika and lightly season with salt.
4. Pan-sear the chicken breasts until they are golden brown on both sides, turning once, about 5 minutes total. Place them in the baking dish and bake until cooked through, about 15 minutes.
5. While the chicken is baking, place a large saucepan filled with water on high heat and bring to a boil. Cook the noodles until al dente according to the package directions. Remove from heat, drain, and stir in the butter and parsley. Season the noodles with salt and pepper.
6. When the chicken is cooked, remove from the oven and let rest for 10 minutes.

REHEATING TIP: To reheat, microwave uncovered for 30-second intervals until heated through. To reheat from frozen, thaw in the refrigerator overnight before reheating as directed.

Per serving: Calories: 515; Total fat: 20g; Saturated fat: 9g; Protein: 39g; Total carbs: 40g; Fiber: 2g; Sugar: 1g; Sodium: 177mg

DAIRY-FREE • VEGAN

ROASTED RED PEPPER SPREAD

SERVINGS: 5 • **PREP TIME:** 10 minutes

Red pepper spread is a popular condiment and snack in many countries around the world. This version is inspired by muhammara, a Middle Eastern dip eaten with pita bread and vegetables and used as a topping on proteins. To make this recipe more traditional, add half a cup of bread crumbs for texture, a couple of tablespoons of pomegranate molasses for flavor, and a teaspoon of red chili flakes for a fiery finish.

2 (6-ounce) jars roasted red peppers, drained

½ cup chopped pecans

2 tablespoons olive oil

Juice of ½ lemon

1½ teaspoons minced garlic

1 teaspoon ground cumin

Sea salt

5 ounces pita chips

1. Place the red peppers, pecans, oil, lemon juice, garlic, and cumin in a blender or food processor and pulse until smooth and well combined.
2. Season with salt and serve with pita chips.

INGREDIENT TIP: You can roast your own red peppers. Place halved, seeded, and lightly oiled peppers in a 450°F oven and roast for 20 minutes until charred and collapsed. Remove from the oven, place in a bowl, cover with plastic wrap, and let sit for 10 minutes to make removing the skin effortless.

Per serving: Calories: 265; Total fat: 17g; Saturated fat: 2g; Protein: 4g; Total carbs: 25g; Fiber: 3g; Sugar: 4g; Sodium: 240mg

CHAPTER 11

Week 11 Prep

Strawberry French Toast Casserole 115

Antipasto Couscous Salad 116

Oktoberfest Soup 117

Lamb Burgers with Tzatziki Sauce 118

Beet and Berry Smoothie 119

As with many other weeks, you'll take a little trip around the world in week 11, sampling dishes inspired by different regions. Enjoy an Italian antipasto salad, a Bavarian soup, and Middle Eastern burgers. The smoothie, baked breakfast casserole, and simple salad make the prep work a snap. With the saved time, you can use a recipe from chapter 16 to make homemade Tzatziki Sauce (page 178) or use store-bought.

Lamb Burgers with Tzatziki Sauce, page 118

SHOPPING LIST

5-INGREDIENT PANTRY

- *Black pepper, freshly ground*
- *Garlic, minced (2 teaspoons)*
- *Nonstick cooking spray*
- *Oil, olive (2 tablespoons)*
- *Onion, red (1)*
- *Onion, sweet (1)*
- *Salt, sea*

MEAT, POULTRY, SEAFOOD

- Italian meats (9 ounces)
- Lamb, ground, extra-lean (12 ounces)
- Sausage, smoked (12 ounces)

DAIRY AND NONDAIRY SUBSTITUTES

- Almond milk, vanilla, unsweetened, 1 (half-gallon) container
- Eggs, large (8)
- Milk, 2 percent (2 cups)
- Tzatziki sauce (¼ cup)

PRODUCE

- Beets (10)
- Cabbage, shredded (4 cups)
- Carrots (2)
- Kale (2½ cups)
- Lettuce, iceberg (1 head)
- Potatoes, russet (2)
- Strawberries (2 cups)
- Tomatoes, cherry (3 cups, or about 20 ounces)

CANNED AND JARRED

- Antipasto, mixed (3 cups)
- Balsamic dressing (½ cup)
- Maple syrup (5 tablespoons)

PANTRY

- Chicken broth, low-sodium (8 cups)
- Couscous (½ cup)
- Vanilla extract, pure (1 tablespoon)

OTHER

- Berries, mixed, frozen (1 [16-ounce] bag)
- Brioche bread (1 [16-ounce] loaf)
- Buns, Kaiser-style, whole-wheat (3)

	BREAKFAST	LUNCH	DINNER	SNACK/DESSERT
DAY 1	Strawberry French Toast Casserole	Antipasto Couscous Salad	Lamb Burgers with Tzatziki Sauce	Beet and Berry Smoothie
DAY 2	Strawberry French Toast Casserole	Antipasto Couscous Salad	Oktoberfest Soup	Beet and Berry Smoothie
DAY 3	Strawberry French Toast Casserole	Antipasto Couscous Salad	Oktoberfest Soup	Beet and Berry Smoothie
DAY 4	Strawberry French Toast Casserole	Oktoberfest Soup	Lamb Burgers with Tzatziki Sauce	Beet and Berry Smoothie
DAY 5	Strawberry French Toast Casserole	Oktoberfest Soup	Lamb Burgers with Tzatziki Sauce	Beet and Berry Smoothie

STEP-BY-STEP PREP

1. Assemble the Strawberry French Toast Casserole (page 115) and refrigerate for 1 hour.

2. Prepare the beets and kale for the Beet and Berry Smoothie (page 119) by spreading the chopped vegetables on the baking sheet and freezing until frozen, about 1 hour.

3. Cook the couscous for the Antipasto Couscous Salad (page 116), divide among 3 large meal prep containers, and set them in the refrigerator to cool.

4. Preheat the oven to 350°F.

5. Prepare the vegetables and sausage for the Oktoberfest Soup (page 117):
    - Chop the sweet onion.
    - Shred the cabbage.
    - Peel and dice the carrots and potatoes.
    - Slice the sausage.
6. Make the Octoberfest soup and put it on to cook.
7. Remove the French toast casserole from the refrigerator and place it in the oven to bake.
8. For the smoothies, transfer the frozen beets and kale from the baking tray and frozen berries from the package to 5 medium sealable bags, evenly dividing the ingredients among each. Seal, label, and place the bags in the freezer for up to 1 month. Evenly divide the almond milk and maple syrup among 5 medium meal prep containers, about 1⅔ cups of almond milk and 1 tablespoon of maple syrup in each, and store in the refrigerator for up to 5 days.
9. Make the Antipasto Couscous Salad recipe completely. Seal, label, and store the salad and dressing containers in the refrigerator for up to 5 days.
10. Portion the soup among 4 large meal prep containers. Seal, label, and store 2 containers in the refrigerator for up to 3 days and 2 containers in the freezer for up to 1 month.
11. When the casserole is done, portion it into 5 large meal prep containers. Seal, label, and store in the refrigerator for up to 5 days.
12. Cook the patties for the Lamb Burgers with Tzatziki Sauce (page 118), then place the patties on one side of 3 large (2-compartment) meal prep containers and place in the refrigerator to cool.
13. While the burgers are cooling, evenly divide the sauce among 3 small (2-ounce) containers, label, and store in the refrigerator for up to 1 week. Place 1 bun each in 3 small sealable plastic bags, label, and refrigerate for up to 5 days. Shred the lettuce and slice the red onion.
14. When the burgers are cool, place the shredded lettuce and sliced red onion in the other compartment of each of the burger containers. Seal, label, and store in the refrigerator for up to 3 days.

NUT-FREE • VEGETARIAN

STRAWBERRY FRENCH TOAST CASSEROLE

SERVINGS: 5 • **PREP TIME:** 15 minutes, plus 1 hour to chill • **COOK TIME:** 45 minutes

French toast is a delightful, decadent breakfast treat. Usually, this egg-dipped bread is fried in a skillet to a perfect golden brown and served with a generous splash of maple syrup. This easy-to-prepare casserole version is baked instead and sweetened with sliced fresh strawberries. Brioche is the best bread for French toast because its tender texture soaks up the egg and becomes almost custard-like when cooked, but you can use any type of soft bread.

Nonstick cooking spray

¾ **loaf brioche or French bread, cut into 1-inch cubes**

2 cups sliced strawberries

8 large eggs

2 cups 2 percent milk

1 tablespoon pure vanilla extract

1. Lightly grease a 9-by-13-inch baking dish with cooking spray.
2. Spread half the bread cubes in the baking dish and top them with half the strawberries. Repeat with the remaining bread and berries.
3. In a medium bowl, whisk together the eggs, milk, and vanilla, and pour the mixture evenly over the bread and berries. Cover and let the casserole sit in the refrigerator for 1 hour.
4. Preheat the oven to 350°F.
5. Bake the casserole uncovered until a knife inserted in the middle comes out clean, about 45 minutes.

REHEATING TIP: To reheat, microwave uncovered for 30-second intervals until heated through.

SERVING TIP: Top with maple syrup, sliced banana, blueberries, lemon zest, or even a bit of chopped chocolate.

Per serving: Calories: 384; Total fat: 13g; Saturated fat: 5g; Protein: 20g; Total carbs: 44g; Fiber: 3g; Sugar: 10g; Sodium: 372mg

DAIRY-FREE

ANTIPASTO COUSCOUS SALAD

SERVINGS: 3 • **PREP TIME:** 15 minutes • **COOK TIME:** 10 minutes

Antipasto is the first course of a traditional Italian meal, featuring platters or bowls of cured meats, olives, cheeses, roasted red peppers, marinated artichoke hearts, and mixed pickles. This salad takes all those assertive flavors and combines them with mild-tasting couscous and fresh tomatoes. Look for packages of classic Italian meats—they often contain three types per package—and jars of mixed antipasto pickles and marinated vegetables to simplify your shopping.

¾ cup water

½ cup couscous

3 cups quartered cherry tomatoes

¼ red onion, thinly sliced

3 cups store-bought jarred mixed antipasto (artichoke hearts, olives, roasted red peppers)

6 ounces mixed Italian meats (prosciutto, Genoa salami, etc.), chopped

½ cup store-bought balsamic dressing or Simple Herbed Balsamic Dressing (page 174)

1. In a medium saucepan over high heat, bring the water to a boil.

2. Remove the saucepan from the heat, stir in the couscous, cover, and set aside for 10 minutes. Fluff the couscous with a fork.

3. When the couscous is cool, divide it among 3 containers and layer the tomatoes, onion, antipasto, and meats into each container.

4. Divide the dressing among 3 (2-ounce) containers.

Per serving: Calories: 488; Total fat: 25g; Saturated fat: 6g; Protein: 19g; Total carbs: 40g; Fiber: 7g; Sugar: 7g; Sodium: 912mg

DAIRY-FREE • GLUTEN-FREE • NUT-FREE

OKTOBERFEST SOUP

SERVINGS: 4 • **PREP TIME:** 15 minutes • **COOK TIME:** 43 minutes

Oktoberfest is a famous Bavarian festival featuring delicious food and, usually, lots of beer! This soup combines some of the culinary elements of Oktoberfest such as sausage, cabbage, and potatoes. Try topping the soup with a generous sprinkling of Gruyère cheese when heating it up.

1 tablespoon olive oil

1 sweet onion, chopped

2 teaspoons minced garlic

1 (12-ounce) smoked sausage, cut into ¼-inch slices

4 cups shredded green cabbage

2 carrots, diced

2 russet potatoes, diced

8 cups low-sodium chicken broth

Sea salt

Freshly ground black pepper

1. In a large stockpot, heat the oil over medium-high heat.
2. Add the onion and garlic. Sauté for about 3 minutes, or until translucent.
3. Add the sausage, cabbage, carrots, potatoes, and broth.
4. Bring the soup to a boil, then reduce the heat to low and simmer until the vegetables are tender, about 40 minutes.
5. Season with salt and pepper.

REHEATING TIP: To reheat, microwave uncovered for 30-second intervals until heated through. To reheat from frozen, thaw in the refrigerator overnight before reheating as directed.

Per serving: Calories: 449; Total fat: 28g; Saturated fat: 9g; Protein: 15g; Total carbs: 36g; Fiber: 5g; Sugar: 9g; Sodium: 521mg

NUT-FREE

LAMB BURGERS with TZATZIKI SAUCE

SERVINGS: 3 • **PREP TIME:** 10 minutes • **COOK TIME:** 12 to 15 minutes

Beef and poultry burgers are common in most households, but lean ground lamb has an incredible flavor and is an excellent source of high-quality protein. You'll notice that these burgers do not include any fillers such as milk, egg, or bread crumbs—this is because lamb has a strong taste that needs nothing other than salt and pepper.

12 ounces extra-lean ground lamb

Sea salt

Freshly ground black pepper

1 tablespoon olive oil

¼ cup store-bought tzatziki sauce or homemade Tzatziki Sauce (page 178)

1½ cups shredded iceberg lettuce

½ red onion, thinly sliced

3 whole-wheat buns

1. Form the lamb into 3 patties, flattening them to about ½-inch thickness. Lightly season the patties with salt and pepper.

2. In a large skillet, heat the oil over medium-high heat and cook the patties until no longer pink, turning once, 12 to 15 minutes total. Remove the patties from the skillet and place them on a plate to cool in the refrigerator. Serve with the tzatziki sauce, lettuce, onion, and buns.

REHEATING TIP: To reheat, microwave the patty for 30-second intervals until heated through and serve on the bun topped with sauce, lettuce, and onion. To reheat from frozen, thaw in the refrigerator overnight before reheating as directed.

Per serving: Calories: 448; Total fat: 29g; Saturated fat: 11g; Protein: 24g; Total carbs: 22g; Fiber: 3g; Sugar: 5g; Sodium: 256mg

DAIRY-FREE • GLUTEN-FREE • VEGAN

BEET *and* BERRY SMOOTHIE

SERVINGS: 5 • **PREP TIME:** 10 minutes, plus 1 hour to freeze

Beets can be intimidating and very messy to prepare because they tend to stain everything they touch. You can purchase packaged, peeled beets if you are concerned about a mess, but the flavor will not be as intense or the color as vibrant. You can also wear gloves when handling the beets or rub your stained hands with fresh lemon juice until they're clean.

10 beets, peeled and diced

2½ cups chopped fresh kale

1 (16-ounce) bag frozen mixed berries

1 (half-gallon) container sweetened vanilla almond or cashew milk

5 tablespoons maple syrup

1. Spread the beets and kale on a baking sheet and freeze until frozen, about 1 hour.

2. Divide the frozen beets, kale, and berries into 5 sealable bags and divide the almond milk and maple syrup into 5 (2-cup) containers.

3. Combine 1 bag of the frozen beets, kale, and berries and 1 container of the milk and maple syrup mixture in a blender and blend until smooth. Add a little water if the texture is too thick.

Per serving: Calories: 304; Total fat: 5g; Saturated fat: 0g; Protein: 5g; Total carbs: 63g; Fiber: 8g; Sugar: 51g; Sodium: 277mg

CHAPTER 12

Week 12 Prep

White Bean Breakfast Burritos 125

Chicken Spinach Chowder 126

Roasted Tofu Acorn Squash Bake 127

Slow Cooker Chipotle Chili 128

Chocolate Mint Mousse 129

Your last week has arrived! Hopefully you have learned a lot and found some recipes along the way that are now favorites. This week has a meal prep staple—a breakfast burrito designed to grab and go. You will enjoy three filling, delicious lunch and dinner recipes featuring a comforting chicken soup, an autumn-inspired vegetarian sheet-pan meal, and a spicy chili. The dessert of the plan is a luscious, rich chocolate mousse that will satisfy all your cravings. So dive in and start cooking!

Roasted Tofu Acorn Squash Bake, page 127

SHOPPING LIST

5-INGREDIENT PANTRY

- *Black pepper, freshly ground*
- *Garlic, minced (3 tablespoons)*
- *Oil, olive (6 tablespoons plus 2 teaspoons)*
- *Onion, sweet (4)*
- *Salt, sea*

MEAT, POULTRY, SEAFOOD

- Chicken, 3 (4-ounce) boneless, skinless breasts
- Turkey, ground, extra-lean (12 ounces)

DAIRY AND NONDAIRY SUBSTITUTES

- Cheese, Mexican blend, shredded (1 cup)
- Cream, heavy (whipping) (½ cup)
- Eggs, large (8)
- Milk, 2 percent (1 cups)
- Tofu, extra-firm (1 [14-ounce] package)
- Tofu, silken (1 [14-ounce] package)

PRODUCE

- Acorn squash (1)
- Baby spinach (2 cups, or about 2¼ ounces)
- Basil (1 bunch)
- Bell pepper, red (1), any color (2)

CANNED AND JARRED

- Kidney beans, red, low-sodium (1 [15-ounce] can)
- Navy beans, low-sodium (1 [15-ounce] can)
- Tomatoes, diced, low-sodium (1 [28-ounce] can)
- White beans, low-sodium (1 [15-ounce] can)

PANTRY

- Chicken broth, low-sodium (6 cups)
- Chili powder, chipotle (3 tablespoons)
- Chocolate, dark (8 ounces)
- Peppermint extract (1 teaspoon)
- Sunflower seeds, roasted, unsalted (⅓ cup)
- Vanilla extract, pure (1 teaspoon)

OTHER

- Tortillas, whole-wheat, 5 (10-inch)
- Vegetables, mixed, frozen (3 cups)

	BREAKFAST	LUNCH	DINNER	SNACK/DESSERT
DAY 1	White Bean Breakfast Burritos	Chicken Spinach Chowder	Roasted Tofu Acorn Squash Bake	Chocolate Mint Mousse
DAY 2	White Bean Breakfast Burritos	Slow Cooker Chipotle Chili	Roasted Tofu Acorn Squash Bake	Chocolate Mint Mousse
DAY 3	White Bean Breakfast Burritos	Chicken Spinach Chowder	Roasted Tofu Acorn Squash Bake	Chocolate Mint Mousse
DAY 4	White Bean Breakfast Burritos	Chicken Spinach Chowder	Slow Cooker Chipotle Chili	Chocolate Mint Mousse
DAY 5	White Bean Breakfast Burritos	Chicken Spinach Chowder	Slow Cooker Chipotle Chili	Chocolate Mint Mousse

STEP-BY-STEP PREP

1. Prepare the Slow Cooker Chipotle Chili (page 128) recipe completely and start the slow cooker.

2. Preheat the oven to 375°F.

3. Assemble the Roasted Tofu Acorn Squash Bake (page 127) and place it in the oven to roast.

4. Prepare the ingredients for the Chicken Spinach Chowder (page 126) recipe and put the soup on.

5. When the squash bake is done, divide the mixture among 3 large containers and sprinkle with basil and sunflower seeds. Set in the refrigerator to cool.

6. Make the Chocolate Mint Mousse (page 129) and evenly divide the pudding among 5 medium containers and set in the refrigerator to cool.

7. When the chowder is done, evenly divide it among 4 large meal prep containers and set in the refrigerator to cool.

8. Make the White Bean Breakfast Burritos (page 125), wrap them in foil, label, and store in the refrigerator for up to 5 days or in the freezer for up to 1 month.

9. When the mousse is cool, seal the containers, label, and store in the refrigerator for up to 5 days.

10. When the chili is done, evenly divide it into 3 large containers and place them in the refrigerator to cool.

11. When the squash mixture is cool, seal, label, and store in the refrigerator for up to 3 days.

12. When the chowder is cool, seal, label, and store 2 containers in the refrigerator for up to 3 days and 2 containers in the freezer for up to 1 month.

13. When the chili is cool, seal the containers, label, and store 1 container in the refrigerator for up to 3 days and 2 containers in the freezer for up to 1 month.

NUT-FREE • VEGETARIAN

WHITE BEAN BREAKFAST BURRITOS

SERVINGS: 5 • **PREP TIME:** 15 minutes • **COOK TIME:** 10 minutes

Southwestern-themed breakfast burritos often mimic huevos rancheros because the traditional combination of eggs, salsa, and cheese is delicious. This version can be rolled in tortillas and eaten without fuss or mess. You can swap the canned beans for seasoned refried beans and add a few slices of jalapeño pepper to increase the heat in this dish.

1 tablespoon olive oil

1 red bell pepper, seeded and chopped

1 sweet onion, chopped

1 teaspoon minced garlic

8 large eggs

Sea salt

Freshly ground black pepper

1 (15-ounce) can low-sodium white beans, drained and rinsed

5 (10-inch) whole-wheat tortillas

1 cup shredded Mexican cheese blend or cheddar cheese

1. In a large skillet, heat the oil over medium-high heat.
2. Sauté the bell pepper, onion, and garlic until softened, about 5 minutes.
3. In a medium bowl, whisk the eggs and lightly season with salt and black pepper.
4. Pour the eggs into the skillet and scramble them until fully cooked, about 5 minutes.
5. Remove the skillet from the heat and gently stir in the beans.
6. Place the tortillas on a clean work surface and evenly divide the scrambled egg mixture among the tortillas. Top with the cheese.
7. Fold the side of the tortilla closest to you over the filling, then the right and left sides over that side. Then roll the tortilla away from you to form a sealed packet.

REHEATING TIP: To reheat, unwrap and microwave for 30-second intervals until heated through. If reheating from frozen, unwrap, and place the burrito on a plate and microwave on defrost for 2 to 3 minutes, turning several times. Then microwave for 30-second intervals until heated through.

Per serving: Calories: 453; Total fat: 21g; Saturated fat: 9g; Protein: 25g; Total carbs: 40g; Fiber: 9g; Sugar: 7g; Sodium: 426mg

GLUTEN-FREE • NUT-FREE

CHICKEN SPINACH CHOWDER

SERVINGS: 4 • **PREP TIME:** 10 minutes • **COOK TIME:** 43 minutes

Chowders are creamy soups that usually contain seafood, but chicken works beautifully as well. This soup blend includes a variety of hearty frozen vegetables, which saves prep time and increases the nutrition content. If you are looking for a dairy-free option but still want the rich, creamy finish, replace the heavy cream with coconut milk.

2 tablespoons olive oil

3 (4-ounce) chicken breasts, cut into ½-inch cubes

1 sweet onion, chopped

1 tablespoon minced garlic

6 cups low-sodium chicken broth

3 cups frozen mixed vegetables (soup blend: carrots, celery, potato, green beans, corn)

2 cups shredded fresh baby spinach

½ cup heavy (whipping) cream

Sea salt

Freshly ground black pepper

1. In a large stockpot, heat the oil over medium-high heat and sauté the chicken until just cooked through, about 10 minutes.
2. Add the onion and garlic and sauté for about 3 minutes or until translucent.
3. Add the broth and bring the soup to a boil.
4. Reduce the heat to low and simmer for about 15 minutes, or until the chicken is fall-apart tender.
5. Add the frozen vegetables and simmer until heated through, about 10 minutes.
6. Remove from heat and stir in the spinach and cream. Season with salt and pepper.

REHEATING TIP: To reheat, microwave uncovered for 30-second intervals until heated through. To reheat from frozen, thaw in the refrigerator overnight before reheating as directed.

Per serving: Calories: 415; Total fat: 26g; Saturated fat: 9g; Protein: 24g; Total carbs: 20g; Fiber: 5g; Sugar: 10g; Sodium: 393mg

DAIRY-FREE • GLUTEN-FREE • NUT-FREE • VEGAN

ROASTED TOFU ACORN SQUASH BAKE

SERVINGS: 3 • **PREP TIME:** 15 minutes • **COOK TIME:** 35 minutes

Acorn squash is a less popular choice for many people because it can be incredibly hard to peel. The trick is to pierce the squash all over with a fork and microwave on high for 2 to 4 minutes, then let it cool until you can handle it and peel with a sharp knife. It is definitely worth the effort because acorn squash has a glorious deep color and a rich, almost sweet flavor.

1 acorn squash, peeled and cut into 1-inch cubes

1 (14-ounce) block extra-firm tofu, drained, pressed, and cut into 1-inch cubes

2 bell peppers (any color), seeded and diced

1 sweet onion, cut into eighths

2 teaspoons minced garlic

3 tablespoons olive oil

Sea salt

Freshly ground black pepper

1½ tablespoons chopped fresh basil

⅓ cup roasted, unsalted sunflower seeds

1. Preheat the oven to 375°F. Line a baking sheet with parchment paper.
2. In a large bowl, toss together the squash, tofu, bell peppers, onion, garlic, and oil until well coated. Spread the mixture evenly onto the baking sheet.
3. Roast the mixture, turning once, until golden and tender, about 35 minutes. Season lightly with salt and black pepper. Top each portion with the basil and sunflower seeds.

REHEATING TIP: To reheat, microwave uncovered for 30-second intervals until heated through.

Per serving: Calories: 478; Total fat: 31g; Saturated fat: 4g; Protein: 21g; Total carbs: 38g; Fiber: 7g; Sugar: 6g; Sodium: 39mg

DAIRY-FREE • GLUTEN-FREE • NUT-FREE

SLOW COOKER CHIPOTLE CHILI

SERVINGS: 3 • **PREP TIME:** 10 minutes • **COOK TIME:** 3 hours

Chili is practically a religion for some enthusiastic home cooks and many professional chefs. Everyone has a slightly different variation on the spices, ingredients, and cooking methods used to create this popular meal. This is a simple chili with a great deal of smoky flavor from the chipotle chili powder. Chipotle peppers are smoke-dried, so they have an unmistakable flavor and are on the milder side, which means this recipe will appeal to almost anyone.

2 teaspoons olive oil

12 ounces extra-lean ground turkey

1 sweet onion, chopped

1 tablespoon minced garlic

1 (28-ounce) can low-sodium diced tomatoes

1 (15-ounce) can low-sodium red kidney beans, with liquid

1 (15-ounce) can low-sodium navy beans, drained and rinsed

3 tablespoons chipotle chili powder

1. In a large skillet, heat the oil over medium-high heat. Brown the turkey until cooked through, stirring to break it up, about 10 minutes.

2. Transfer the turkey to the slow cooker, add the onion, garlic, tomatoes, kidney beans, navy beans, and chili powder, and stir to combine.

3. Cover and cook on low for about 3 hours, until the chili is thick.

REHEATING TIP: To reheat, microwave uncovered for 30-second intervals until heated through. To reheat from frozen, thaw in the refrigerator overnight before reheating as directed.

SERVING TIP: Top the chili with cheese, yogurt, sour cream, jalapeño peppers, or crushed tortilla chips for added flavor and texture.

Per serving: Calories: 492; Total fat: 8g; Saturated fat: 2g; Protein: 46g; Total carbs: 66g; Fiber: 26g; Sugar: 17g; Sodium: 234mg

GLUTEN-FREE • NUT-FREE • VEGETARIAN

CHOCOLATE MINT MOUSSE

SERVINGS: 5 • **PREP TIME:** 10 minutes • **COOK TIME:** 10 minutes

If you are a stickler for recipe precision, this is not technically a mousse because it does not include beaten egg yolks and fluffy egg whites carefully folded in. However, the texture is very light and creamy, so it isn't really a pudding either. This simple, luscious snack is combined in a blender, so it only takes about 20 minutes from start to finish.

8 ounces high-quality dark chocolate, finely chopped

1 cup 2 percent milk

1 teaspoon pure vanilla extract

1 (14-ounce) package silken tofu, drained well

1 teaspoon peppermint extract

1. Place the chopped chocolate in a medium bowl and set aside.
2. In a small saucepan, bring the milk and vanilla to a gentle boil over medium-high heat. Remove from heat and pour the milk mixture over the chocolate.
3. Let the mixture stand for about 10 minutes, then whisk until very smooth.
4. Place the tofu into a blender or food processor and blend until smooth, about 20 seconds.
5. Add the melted chocolate mixture and peppermint extract to the blender or food processor and blend until very smooth.

Per serving: Calories: 342; Total fat: 23g; Saturated fat: 11g; Protein: 10g; Total carbs: 25g; Fiber: 5g; Sugar: 14g; Sodium: 37mg

Turkey Taco Stuffed Baked Potatoes, page 154

PART II:
Bonus MEAL PREP Recipes

CHAPTER 13

Breakfast

Chocolate Hazelnut Steel-Cut Oats 134

Veggie and Feta Egg Sandwich 135

Banana Walnut Couscous 136

Quinoa Pecan Granola 137

Lemon Pancakes 138

Sheet-Pan Country Breakfast 139

Savory Farro Breakfast Bowl 140

Ham and Cheese Breakfast Casserole 141

Canadian Bacon and Goat Cheese Egg Muffins 142

Brussels Sprout Egg Skillet 143

Veggie and Feta Egg Sandwich, page 135

GLUTEN-FREE • VEGETARIAN

CHOCOLATE HAZELNUT STEEL-CUT OATS

SERVINGS: 5 • **PREP TIME:** 10 minutes • **COOK TIME:** 25 minutes

The pairing of chocolate and hazelnut is a favorite for many people, as evidenced by the popularity of Nutella that combines these two ingredients. This breakfast has just the right amount of sweetness, but if you have more of a sweet tooth, you can certainly sprinkle a little more sugar on the top of the porridge before digging in.

3 cups water

1 cup milk or nondairy milk, plus extra for serving

3 tablespoons cocoa powder

¼ cup brown sugar

1 cup steel-cut oats

Dash salt

½ cup chopped hazelnuts

1. In a large saucepan, whisk together the water, milk, cocoa, and brown sugar over medium heat. Bring the mixture to a simmer and stir in the oats and salt.

2. Reduce the heat to low and simmer until thick and creamy, stirring occasionally, about 25 minutes.

3. Divide the oats among 5 medium meal prep containers and top with the chopped hazelnuts. Place the containers in the refrigerator to cool.

4. When cool, seal, label, and store in the refrigerator for up to 5 days.

REHEATING TIP: To reheat, microwave uncovered for 30-second intervals until heated through. Add more milk if the texture is too thick.

Per serving: Calories: 265; Total fat: 12g; Saturated fat: 2g; Protein: 9g; Total carbs: 34g; Fiber: 6g; Sugar: 10g; Sodium: 57mg

NUT-FREE • VEGETARIAN

VEGGIE and FETA EGG SANDWICH

SERVINGS: 5 • **PREP TIME:** 10 minutes • **COOK TIME:** 20 to 25 minutes

Make-ahead breakfast sandwiches are the base recipe for many meal prep menus because they are simple and inexpensive and the quality of the meal is unaffected by storage or freezing. Almost any combination of ingredients can be combined for the egg portion; in this case, feta and an assortment of vegetables provide flavor and a pop of color. Feta is naturally salty, so you won't be adding any extra salt to the sandwich.

Nonstick cooking spray

1½ cups mixed frozen vegetables (onion, bell pepper, carrot, corn, green bean), thawed

8 large eggs

1 cup crumbled feta cheese

5 whole-wheat English muffins, cut in half

Freshly ground black pepper

1. Preheat the oven to 350°F.
2. Lightly grease 10 muffin cups in a muffin pan with cooking spray.
3. Evenly divide the thawed vegetables among the cups.
4. In a medium bowl, whisk the eggs, then divide the eggs among the muffin cups, gently shaking the pan to disperse the eggs. Sprinkle the tops with the cheese.
5. Bake until the eggs are cooked through and the tops are lightly golden, 20 to 25 minutes.
6. Place two egg portions on one half of an English muffin, lightly season each with pepper, and top with the other English muffin half.
7. Place each sandwich in a small sealable plastic bag, squeeze out the air, and seal. Label the sandwiches and store in the refrigerator for up to 5 days or in the freezer for up to 2 months.

REHEATING TIP: To reheat, wrap the sandwich in a paper towel and microwave for 30 to 45 seconds.

COOKING TIP: If you don't have a muffin pan, combine all the ingredients in a 9-inch square baking dish and bake for 30 to 35 minutes. Cool and cut the egg mixture into 9 squares and store as directed.

Per serving: Calories: 369; Total fat: 16g; Saturated fat: 7g; Protein: 22g; Total carbs: 36g; Fiber: 7g; Sugar: 7g; Sodium: 453mg

VEGETARIAN

BANANA WALNUT COUSCOUS

SERVINGS: 5 • **PREP TIME:** 5 minutes • **COOK TIME:** 15 minutes

Couscous is a staple ingredient in Middle Eastern cuisine and very simple to prepare. This product looks like a grain but is actually pasta created by hand-rolling and tossing water and semolina together to form tiny balls. The flavor is mild enough to combine well with many different ingredients, both savory and sweet. Couscous is also ideal for storing because it does not get soggy or mushy as it sits or when reheated.

1½ cups water

1 cup milk or nondairy milk, plus extra for serving

1¼ cups couscous

2 bananas

¼ cup maple syrup

½ cup chopped pecans

1. In a large saucepan, stir together the water and milk over medium heat. Bring to a boil.
2. Remove the saucepan from the heat, stir in the couscous, cover, and let stand for 10 minutes.
3. In a small bowl, mash the bananas with a potato masher.
4. Gently fluff the couscous with a fork and stir in the mashed banana and maple syrup.
5. Divide the couscous among 5 medium meal prep containers and top with the chopped pecans. Place the containers in the refrigerator to cool.
6. When cool, seal, label, and store in the refrigerator for up to 5 days.

REHEATING TIP: To reheat, microwave uncovered for 30-second intervals until heated through. Add more milk if the texture is too thick.

Per serving: Calories: 227; Total fat: 9g; Saturated fat: 1g; Protein: 5g; Total carbs: 34g; Fiber: 3g; Sugar: 18g; Sodium: 27mg

DAIRY-FREE • GLUTEN-FREE • VEGAN

QUINOA PECAN GRANOLA

SERVINGS: 5 • **PREP TIME:** 10 minutes • **COOK TIME:** 25 minutes

Homemade granola has many benefits over store-bought products—you can control the sugar, sodium, and allergens when putting together your own. For example, if you have a nut allergy, leave out the pecans and add sunflower or pumpkin seeds instead. If you have a sweet tooth, substitute sweetened coconut flakes for the unsweetened coconut flakes or add a cup of golden raisins after the granola is cooled. The recipe is basically a blank culinary canvas.

- 1½ cups rolled oats
- 1 cup quinoa
- ½ cup chopped pecans
- ¼ cup maple syrup
- 3 tablespoons coconut oil
- ⅛ teaspoon sea salt
- ½ cup **coconut flakes, unsweetened**

1. Preheat the oven to 350°F. Line a baking sheet with parchment paper.
2. In a large bowl, toss together the oats, quinoa, and pecans until well mixed. Add the maple syrup, coconut oil, and salt and toss to coat all ingredients evenly.
3. Spread the mixture on the baking sheet and bake until golden and crispy, about 20 minutes. Evenly scatter the coconut flakes on top and bake for 5 minutes longer.
4. Remove the baking sheet from the oven and let cool for 15 minutes, then break the granola into chunks.
5. Evenly divide the granola among 5 medium meal prep containers and store at room temperature for up to 1 week. Serve with milk or yogurt.

SUBSTITUTION TIP: If you are not a fan of quinoa, double the oats or replace with chia seeds instead.

Per serving: Calories: 515; Total fat: 23g; Saturated fat: 10g; Protein: 14g; Total carbs: 65g; Fiber: 9g; Sugar: 10g; Sodium: 68mg

NUT-FREE • VEGETARIAN

LEMON PANCAKES

SERVINGS: 5 • **PREP TIME:** 10 minutes • **COOK TIME:** 20 minutes

Pancakes always seem like a decadent choice for breakfast—more like dessert than a sensible meal. This might be because the traditional sweet, rich toppings include maple syrup, whipped cream, chocolate, fruit sauces, and butter. This recipe uses citrus and a drizzle of maple syrup for flavor and is low in saturated fat and calories. Try other citrus fruit such as lime or orange if you do not have lemons.

2 cups milk

2 large eggs

Juice and zest of 1 lemon

2¼ cups white self-rising flour

Nonstick cooking spray

Maple syrup, for serving

1. In a large bowl, whisk together the milk, eggs, lemon juice, and lemon zest until well blended. Whisk in the flour until the batter is combined.

2. Heat a large skillet over medium-high heat and lightly grease it with cooking spray.

3. Scoop about ¼ cup of batter per pancake into the skillet and cook until the bubbles on the surface burst, about 2 minutes.

4. Flip the pancakes and cook for 1 to 2 minutes longer until browned on both sides.

5. Repeat with the remaining batter. You should have 15 pancakes.

6. Cool the pancakes completely.

7. Place 3 cooled pancakes in each of 5 medium containers. Pour the maple syrup into 5 (2-ounce) containers and seal them. Label all the containers and store them in the refrigerator for up to 5 days.

REHEATING TIP: Eat the pancakes warm or cold. To reheat, wrap the pancakes in a paper towel and microwave for 30 seconds.

Per serving: Calories: 314; Total sat: 3g; Saturated sat: 1g; Protein: 11g; Total carbs: 58g; Fiber: 2g; Sugar: 16g; Sodium: 514mg

DAIRY-FREE • GLUTEN-FREE • NUT-FREE

SHEET-PAN COUNTRY BREAKFAST

SERVINGS: 5 • **PREP TIME:** 15 minutes • **COOK TIME:** 30 minutes

A hearty country-style breakfast doesn't have to be fat-laden and overly filling; this version includes many elements you might find on a heaping plate in a diner or family restaurant—potatoes, peppers, and tasty sausage. You can also add a can of drained and rinsed navy beans to the other ingredients 10 minutes before the cooking time is complete to increase the fiber and protein.

2 large sweet potatoes, cut into ¾-inch chunks

2 large russet potatoes, cut into ¾-inch chunks

2 red bell peppers, seeded and cut into 1½-inch chunks

1 tablespoon olive oil

Sea salt

Freshly ground black pepper

1 pound breakfast sausages

2 scallions, white and green parts, chopped

1. Preheat the oven to 400°F. Line a baking sheet with parchment paper.

2. In a large bowl, toss together the sweet potatoes, russet potatoes, and bell peppers with the oil to coat evenly. Season with salt and black pepper.

3. Spread the vegetables on two-thirds of the baking sheet and the sausages on the remaining third. Prick the sausages all over with a fork.

4. Roast until the sausages are cooked through and the vegetables are golden and tender, turning once halfway through, about 30 minutes.

5. Divide the vegetables and sausages among 5 large meal prep containers and set in the refrigerator to cool.

6. When cool, top with the scallions, seal, label, and store in the refrigerator for up to 5 days.

REHEATING TIP: To reheat, microwave uncovered for 30-second intervals until heated through.

Per serving: Calories: 466; Total fat: 31g; Saturated fat: 10g; Protein: 16g; Total carbs: 30g; Fiber: 4g; Sugar: 5g; Sodium: 599mg

NUT-FREE • VEGETARIAN

SAVORY FARRO BREAKFAST BOWL

SERVINGS: 5 • **PREP TIME:** 15 minutes • **COOK TIME:** 20 minutes

Breakfast bowls can be sweet fruit- and nut-topped creations or savory veggie- and egg-packed meals. This is a savory recipe, combining tender grains, fiber-packed broccoli and tomatoes, and protein-rich eggs for a balanced, filling meal. If you have a heavily scheduled week coming up, this is the perfect breakfast for your meal prep menu. You can eat it hot or cold, and your energy levels will stay high all morning.

1¼ cups farro

2½ cups water

3 teaspoons olive oil, divided

2 cups broccoli slaw

½ sweet onion, chopped

1 teaspoon minced garlic

10 large eggs

Sea salt

Freshly ground black pepper

2 cups halved cherry tomatoes

1 cup shredded Swiss cheese or any sharp cheese

1. In a medium saucepan, combine the farro and water and bring to a boil over medium-high heat. Cover, reduce the heat, and simmer until the grains are tender and the water is absorbed, about 20 minutes.

2. While the farro is cooking, heat 2 teaspoons of oil in a large skillet and sauté the broccoli slaw, onion, and garlic until tender, about 10 minutes. Remove the vegetables and set aside.

3. Wipe out the skillet and heat the remaining 1 teaspoon of oil over medium heat.

4. In a medium bowl, whisk the eggs and season lightly with salt and pepper. Pour the eggs into the skillet and scramble the eggs until just cooked through, about 5 minutes. Remove the skillet from the heat.

5. Evenly divide the farro, eggs, vegetables, tomatoes, and cheese among 5 large meal prep containers and place them in the refrigerator to cool.

6. When cool, seal, label, and store in the refrigerator for up to 5 days.

Per serving: Calories: 403; Total fat: 19g; Saturated fat: 7g; Protein: 24g; Total carbs: 36g; Fiber: 6g; Sugar: 5g; Sodium: 181mg

GLUTEN-FREE • NUT-FREE

HAM and CHEESE BREAKFAST CASSEROLE

SERVINGS: 5 • **PREP TIME:** 10 minutes • **COOK TIME:** 53 minutes

Ham and cheese is a classic combination found in sandwiches, on pizza, and in tempting casseroles of all kinds. Kale adds an attractive color and a pleasing earthy taste to this dish, and it is one of the most nutrition-dense foods you can eat, as it is high in vitamins K and C and antioxidants.

Nonstick cooking spray

1 tablespoon olive oil

2 cups sliced white mushrooms

1 sweet onion, chopped

2 teaspoons minced garlic

1 cup shredded fresh kale

½ pound chopped lean ham

8 large eggs

¼ teaspoon sea salt

⅛ teaspoon freshly ground black pepper

¾ cup shredded cheddar cheese

1. Preheat the oven to 350°F. Line a 9-inch square baking dish with parchment paper and grease it with cooking spray.

2. In a large skillet, heat the oil over medium-high heat. Add the mushrooms, onion, and garlic and sauté until the vegetables are tender, about 6 minutes.

3. Add the kale and sauté for 2 minutes.

4. Transfer the mixture to the baking dish and spread it evenly. Evenly spread the ham over the vegetables.

5. In a medium bowl, whisk the eggs, salt, and pepper. Pour the eggs into the baking dish and tap the dish lightly on the counter to disperse the eggs. Sprinkle with the cheese.

6. Bake until the casserole is just cooked through and lightly browned on top, about 45 minutes.

7. Remove the casserole from the oven, cool for 10 minutes, and cut into 5 portions.

8. Transfer the portions to 5 medium containers and place them in the refrigerator to cool completely.

9. Seal, label, and store in the refrigerator for up to 5 days.

REHEATING TIP: Eat this meal cold or warm. To reheat, microwave uncovered for 45 to 60 seconds.

Per serving: Calories: 301; Total fat: 18g; Saturated fat: 7g; Protein: 25g; Total carbs: 8g; Fiber: 1g; Sugar: 5g; Sodium: 676mg

GLUTEN-FREE • NUT-FREE

CANADIAN BACON and GOAT CHEESE EGG MUFFINS

SERVINGS: 5 • **PREP TIME:** 10 minutes • **COOK TIME:** 25 to 30 minutes

Canadian bacon is lean and remains juicy when cooked. If you can't find it, regular bacon works too. The shredded zucchini ensures the muffins don't dry out when cooking or reheating. Feel free to use yellow summer squash instead of zucchini.

Nonstick cooking spray

4 slices Canadian bacon

2 zucchini, shredded

1 large red bell pepper, chopped

8 large eggs

⅛ teaspoon sea salt

⅛ teaspoon freshly ground black pepper

1 cup crumbled goat cheese

1. Preheat the oven to 350°F.
2. Lightly grease 10 muffin cups in a muffin pan with cooking spray.
3. Lightly grease a medium skillet with cooking spray and place it on medium-high heat. Fry the bacon until cooked through, turning once, about 5 minutes. Remove the bacon to a cutting board and chop.
4. Evenly divide the bacon, zucchini, and bell pepper among the muffin cups.
5. In a medium bowl, whisk the eggs, salt, and black pepper and divide the eggs among the muffin cups, gently shaking the pan to disperse the eggs. Sprinkle the tops with the cheese.
6. Bake the egg muffins until they are cooked through and the tops are lightly golden, 20 to 25 minutes.
7. Let the muffins stand 10 minutes, then remove from the muffin tin. Cool in the refrigerator.
8. Place 2 muffins each in 5 medium sealable plastic bags, squeeze out the air, seal, label and store in the refrigerator for up to 5 days or in the freezer for up to 2 months.

REHEATING TIP: Eat this meal cold or warm. To reheat, microwave uncovered for 30 to 45 seconds.

Per serving: Calories: 236; Total fat: 14g; Saturated fat: 6g; Protein: 20g; Total carbs: 6g; Fiber: 2g; Sugar: 4g; Sodium: 436mg

DAIRY-FREE • GLUTEN-FREE • NUT-FREE

BRUSSELS SPROUT EGG SKILLET

SERVINGS: 5 • **PREP TIME:** 15 minutes • **COOK TIME:** 26 minutes

Brussels sprouts are often overlooked in the produce section because they seem complicated to prepare, and their family members cauliflower and broccoli are more familiar. Brussels sprouts do need to be cleaned very well, so leave a little extra time in your cooking schedule for this task. It's worth the effort because this hearty vegetable can be stored and frozen with no loss of texture.

- **10 bacon slices, chopped**
- **4 cups quartered Brussels sprouts**
- ½ sweet onion, chopped
- 2 teaspoons minced garlic
- **1 carrot, peeled and shredded**
- **1 teaspoon dried thyme**
- **10 large eggs**
- Sea salt
- Freshly ground black pepper

1. In a large skillet over medium-high heat, sauté the bacon until cooked through and crispy, about 6 minutes. Remove the bacon to a plate and set aside. Drain off all the bacon fat except 1 tablespoon.
2. In the same skillet, sauté the Brussels sprouts, onion, and garlic until tender, about 10 minutes. Add the carrot and sauté for 2 minutes longer.
3. Add the bacon back to the skillet with the thyme, stirring to combine.
4. In a medium bowl, whisk the eggs and pour them into the skillet, shaking to disperse.
5. Cook the eggs, lifting the edges to let the uncooked egg flow under the cooked portions, until the bottom is set and the top is cooked through, about 8 minutes. Season with salt and pepper.
6. Divide into 5 equal portions, transfer to 5 large meal prep containers, and place them in the refrigerator to cool.
7. When cool, seal, label, and store in the refrigerator for up to 5 days.

REHEATING TIP: Eat this meal cold or warm. To reheat, microwave uncovered for 30-second intervals until heated through.

Per serving: Calories: 285; Total fat: 17g; Saturated fat: 5g; Protein: 21g; Total carbs: 13g; Fiber: 4g; Sugar: 5g; Sodium: 435mg

CHAPTER 14

Lunch and Dinner

Sweet Potato Tabbouleh 146

Southwest Broccoli Salad 147

Chicken Caprese Salad 148

Noodle Bowls with Peanut Sauce 149

Chickpea Root Vegetable Curry 150

Hoisin Salmon with Bok Choy 151

Balsamic-Marinated Halibut with Farro 152

Chicken Pesto Penne 153

Turkey Taco Stuffed Baked Potatoes 154

Shawarma-Rubbed Pork Sheet-Pan Dinner 155

Beef-Stuffed Squash 156

Sheet-Pan Beef Fajitas 157

Savory Farro Breakfast Bowl, page 140

DAIRY-FREE • NUT-FREE • VEGAN

SWEET POTATO TABBOULEH

SERVINGS: 3 • **PREP TIME:** 20 minutes • **COOK TIME:** 25 minutes

Salads are fabulous for meal prep because they usually take less time to throw together on your cooking day and don't have to be reheated. A grain-based salad is an excellent choice because it is very filling and you don't have to worry about wilted greens at the end of a five-day menu. Tabbouleh is packed with vegetables, and the simple balsamic dressing in this version adds just the right amount of tartness. For added crunch, sprinkle with toasted pumpkin seeds or a scattering of chopped pecans.

2 teaspoons olive oil

2 sweet potatoes, cut into ½-inch cubes

Sea salt

1 cup water

½ cup bulgur

2 red bell peppers, seeded and chopped

¼ red onion, chopped

½ cup store-bought balsamic dressing or Simple Herbed Balsamic Dressing (page 174)

¼ cup chopped fresh parsley

1. Preheat the oven to 425°F. Line a baking sheet with parchment paper.

2. In a medium bowl, toss together the oil and sweet potatoes and season with salt. Spread the potatoes on the baking sheet and roast until tender, turning once, about 25 minutes. Remove the baking sheet from the oven and transfer the sweet potatoes to a large bowl.

3. While the potatoes are baking, in a small saucepan, bring the water to a boil over medium-high heat. Stir in the bulgur, cover, reduce the heat to medium-low, and simmer until tender and the liquid is absorbed, about 12 minutes. Remove from heat and set aside covered for 10 minutes.

4. Add the bulgur to the bowl with the sweet potatoes along with the peppers, onion, dressing, and parsley. Toss to combine.

5. Evenly divide the tabbouleh among 3 large meal prep containers and place in the refrigerator to cool.

6. When cool, seal, label, and store in the refrigerator for up to 4 days.

Per serving: Calories: 305; Total fat: 12g; Saturated fat: 2g; Protein: 5g; Total carbs: 46g; Fiber: 8g; Sugar: 12g; Sodium: 347mg

GLUTEN-FREE • NUT-FREE

SOUTHWEST BROCCOLI SALAD

SERVINGS: 4 • **PREP TIME:** 20 minutes

Southwest flavors are complex and usually deliver a bit of heat. This is a milder salad, but you can add a scoop of salsa or top with jalapeño peppers for an extra kick. Chopped broccoli is firm and the florets hold the dressing wonderfully, so it is a perfect salad base. Try tucking the salad into a tortilla for a healthy wrap you can eat on the go.

- **½ cup salsa ranch dressing**
- **1 (15-ounce) can sodium-free black beans, drained and rinsed**
- **8 cups chopped broccoli**
- **2 bell peppers, any color, seeded and diced**
- **1 cup fresh corn kernels**
- ½ red onion, thinly sliced

1. Divide the dressing among 4 large meal prep containers. Layer the black beans, broccoli, peppers, corn, and red onion into each container, dividing the ingredients evenly.

2. Seal the containers, label, and store in the refrigerator for up to 5 days.

Per serving: Calories: 349; Total fat: 15g; Saturated fat: 2g; Protein: 14g; Total carbs: 47g; Fiber: 13g; Sugar: 5g; Sodium: 337mg

GLUTEN-FREE • NUT-FREE

CHICKEN CAPRESE SALAD

SERVINGS: 3 • **PREP TIME:** 10 minutes • **COOK TIME:** 15 minutes

Caprese is a patriotic salad meant to mimic the colors of the Italian flag—green, white, and red. These flavors are fresh and clean with sweet tomatoes, creamy mozzarella, and tart balsamic vinegar. Although romaine is an excellent addition, you can also add a cooked whole-grain pasta and prepare the salad as directed. Both versions hold up well for the week.

3 (4-ounce) boneless, skinless chicken breasts, diced

Sea salt

Freshly ground black pepper

1 tablespoon olive oil

6 tablespoons store-bought balsamic dressing or Simple Herbed Balsamic Dressing (page 174)

3 cups halved cherry tomatoes

3 ounces diced whole-milk mozzarella

6 cups chopped romaine lettuce

1. Season the chicken with salt and pepper.
2. In a large skillet, heat the oil over medium-high heat and sauté the chicken until cooked through, about 15 minutes.
3. Remove the chicken from the skillet to a plate, place in the refrigerator, and cool completely.
4. Divide the dressing among 3 large meal prep containers. Layer the chicken, tomatoes, and mozzarella into each container, dividing the ingredients evenly. Top each salad with 2 cups of lettuce.
5. Seal the containers, label, and store in the refrigerator for up to 5 days.

INGREDIENT TIP: Add some fresh basil leaves to the dish to create a more traditional Caprese salad. This herb can be found in most grocery stores but does not have a long shelf life, so do not mix the basil into the salad until just before serving.

Per serving: Calories: 362; Total fat: 19g; Saturated fat: 6g; Protein: 34g; Total carbs: 13g; Fiber: 4g; Sugar: 9g; Sodium: 443mg

DAIRY-FREE • GLUTEN-FREE • VEGETARIAN

NOODLE BOWLS with PEANUT SAUCE

SERVINGS: 3 • **PREP TIME:** 20 minutes • **COOK TIME:** 10 minutes

If you frequent Thai restaurants, there is an excellent chance you have ordered pad Thai, an extremely popular take-out dish and street food. This version is not a classic pad Thai recipe but it tastes similar. Try adding julienned green mango, shredded bok choy, and chopped peanuts or cashews to jazz it up. You can also include a sprinkle of red pepper flakes or chopped jalapeño peppers for a fiery variation.

- 1 (8-ounce) package rice noodles
- 1 (16-ounce) package shredded coleslaw mix
- 2 red bell peppers, seeded and julienned
- 2 cups fresh snow peas, stems and strings removed, julienned
- ¾ cup store-bought peanut dressing or Creamy Peanut Dressing (page 176)

1. Place the rice noodles in a large bowl.
2. In a large saucepan, bring water to a boil over high heat. Pour the boiling water over the rice noodles to cover completely. Let sit for about 10 minutes, stirring 3 to 4 times, until tender and cooked. Drain the noodles and return them to the bowl.
3. Add the coleslaw mix, peppers, and snow peas, and toss to combine. Add the dressing and toss.
4. Evenly divide the recipe among 3 large meal prep containers. Seal, label, and store in the refrigerator for up to 5 days.

Per serving: Calories: 511; Total fat: 12g; Saturated fat: 2g; Protein: 12g; Total carbs: 87g; Fiber: 7g; Sugar: 19g; Sodium: 563mg

DAIRY-FREE • GLUTEN-FREE • NUT-FREE • VEGAN

CHICKPEA ROOT VEGETABLE CURRY

SERVINGS: 3 • **PREP TIME:** 15 minutes • **COOK TIME:** 20 minutes

Curry recipes can range from mild and creamy to mouth-scorching. The heat in this version depends entirely on the type of curry you add. For a tomato-based sauce, add a can of crushed tomatoes; for a creamy base, throw in a can of full-fat coconut milk. These additions will increase your servings to four portions.

½ cup white rice

1 cup water

1 tablespoon olive oil

1 sweet onion, chopped

2 teaspoons minced garlic

2 tablespoons curry powder or paste, mild or hot

2 sweet potatoes, cut into 1-inch chunks

2 parsnips, cut into 1-inch chunks

1 (15-ounce) can no-salt-added chickpeas, liquid reserved

1. In a medium saucepan over medium-high heat, stir together the rice and water and bring to a boil. Reduce the heat to low, cover, and simmer until the liquid is absorbed and the rice is tender, about 20 minutes. Remove from heat and set aside.

2. While the rice is cooking, in a large skillet, heat the oil over medium-high heat. Sauté the onion and garlic until softened, about 2 minutes. Add the curry powder and sauté for 1 additional minute.

3. Add the sweet potatoes, parsnips, and chickpeas with their liquid and bring to a boil. Reduce the heat to low and simmer until the vegetables are tender, about 15 minutes, adding a little water if the consistency is too thick.

4. Evenly divide the rice into the larger compartment of 3 large (2-compartment) meal prep containers. Evenly divide the curry among the empty compartments.

5. Cool the meals in the refrigerator. When cool, seal, label, and store in the refrigerator for up to 5 days.

COOKING TIP: You can make this in a slow cooker if you want to set it and forget it. Combine all the ingredients except the rice in the insert and cook on low for 2 to 3 hours. Cook the rice separately and serve together when finished.

Per serving: Calories: 480; Total fat: 8g; Saturated fat: 1g; Protein: 13g; Total carbs: 91g; Fiber: 17g; Sugar: 17g; Sodium: 79mg

DAIRY-FREE • NUT-FREE

HOISIN SALMON with BOK CHOY

SERVINGS: 3 • **PREP TIME:** 10 minutes, plus 30 minutes marinating time • **COOK TIME:** 20 minutes

The complexity of hoisin sauce makes it a fabulous choice for many recipes, combining spicy, sweet, and tangy flavors perfectly. If you have an issue with gluten, check the label of the sauce because some products are not gluten-free.

3 (4-ounce) salmon fillets

½ cup store-bought hoisin dressing or Hoisin Dressing and Marinade (page 175)

½ cup white rice

1 cup water

6 baby bok choy

1 tablespoon olive oil

Sea salt

Freshly ground black pepper

2 tablespoons toasted sesame seeds

1. In a small bowl, marinate the salmon with the hoisin dressing and refrigerate covered for 30 minutes

2. Preheat the oven to 400°F. Line a baking sheet with parchment paper.

3. In a medium saucepan over medium-high heat, stir together the rice and water and bring to a boil. Reduce the heat to low, cover, and simmer until the liquid is absorbed and the rice is tender, about 20 minutes. Remove from heat and set aside.

4. While the rice is cooking, take the fish out of the marinade and place the fillets on one-half of the baking sheet.

5. In a medium bowl, toss the bok choy with the oil and lightly season with salt and pepper. Spread the bok choy on the empty one-half of the baking sheet.

6. Bake the fish and vegetables for 10 to 12 minutes, or until the fish flakes easily with a fork. Remove from the oven.

7. Evenly divide the rice, salmon, and bok choy among 3 large (3-compartment) containers. Top each serving of the fish and bok choy evenly with the sesame seeds and place the containers in the refrigerator to cool completely.

8. Seal, label, and store in the refrigerator for up to 4 days.

REHEATING TIP: To reheat, microwave uncovered for 30-second intervals until heated through.

Per serving: Calories: 477; Total fat: 16g; Saturated fat: 2g; Protein: 29g; Total carbs: 54g; Fiber: 6g; Sugar: 16g; Sodium: 587mg

DAIRY-FREE • GLUTEN-FREE • NUT-FREE

BALSAMIC-MARINATED HALIBUT with FARRO

SERVINGS: 3 • **PREP TIME:** 15 minutes, plus 30 minutes marinating time • **COOK TIME:** 23 minutes

Fish cooks very well on a sheet pan. When adding vegetables, make sure they have a similar roasting time as the fish so that everything cooks evenly. Look for tender vegetables such as the green beans in this recipe or snow peas, bell peppers, asparagus, zucchini, or some dark leafy greens. If you use more robust vegetables, cut them into small pieces to reduce the time they need in the oven.

3 (5-ounce) halibut fillets

¾ cup store-bought balsamic dressing or Simple Herbed Balsamic Dressing (page 174), divided

1 teaspoon olive oil

¼ sweet onion, chopped

¾ cup farro

1½ cups low-sodium chicken broth

1 pound green beans

1. In a medium bowl, marinate the halibut with ½ cup of balsamic dressing and refrigerate covered for 30 minutes.

2. Preheat the oven to 350°F. Line a baking sheet with parchment paper.

3. In a medium saucepan, heat the oil over medium-high heat. Add the onion and sauté the onion until tender, about 3 minutes. Add the farro and broth and bring to a boil. Cover, reduce the heat, and simmer until the grains are tender and the broth is absorbed, about 20 minutes.

4. While the farro is cooking, toss the remaining ¼ cup of balsamic dressing with the green beans in a medium bowl and spread the beans on two-thirds of the baking sheet. Transfer the fish to the remaining one-third of the baking sheet.

5. Bake until the fish flakes when pressed lightly and the beans are tender and lightly caramelized, about 20 minutes.

6. Evenly divide the farro, halibut, and beans among 3 large (3-compartment) meal prep containers. Place the containers in the refrigerator to cool completely.

7. Seal, label, and store for up to 4 days.

REHEATING TIP: To reheat, microwave uncovered for 30-second intervals until heated through.

Per serving: Calories: 377; Total fat: 9g; Saturated fat: 2g; Protein: 34g; Total carbs: 42g; Fiber: 9g; Sugar: 9g; Sodium: 325mg

CHICKEN PESTO PENNE

SERVINGS: 4 • **PREP TIME:** 10 minutes • **COOK TIME:** 32 minutes

Pasta is an often-used choice in meal prep because it holds up extremely well in the refrigerator. Pesto provides a burst of intense flavor, and when combined with tender chicken and the spinach, you have a restaurant-quality meal. Try regular basil pesto or even black olive tapenade for different flavor variations of this dish.

Nonstick cooking spray

8 ounces dry whole-grain penne

4 cups fresh baby spinach

1 tablespoon olive oil

4 (4-ounce) boneless, skinless chicken breasts, cut into 1-inch chunks

1 cup store-bought sun-dried tomato pesto

¾ cup grated Parmesan cheese

1. Preheat the oven to 350°F. Lightly grease a 9-by-13-inch casserole dish with cooking spray.

2. Place a medium saucepan filled with water on high heat and bring to a boil. Cook the penne until al dente according to the package directions. Remove from heat and stir the spinach into the penne and hot water and let stand for 3 minutes. Reserve ½ cup of the cooking liquid and set aside. Drain the penne and spinach and rinse in cool water.

3. While the penne is cooking, in a large skillet, heat the oil over medium-high heat and sauté the chicken until cooked through, 5 to 6 minutes. Remove from heat.

4. Add the penne, spinach, and pesto to the chicken and toss to coat, adding some of the cooking liquid to create a velvety sauce.

5. Transfer the mixture to the casserole dish and sprinkle with the cheese.

6. Bake until heated through and lightly browned, about 20 minutes.

7. Transfer the penne to 4 large meal prep containers. Cover, label, and store in the refrigerator for up to 5 days.

REHEATING TIP: To reheat, microwave for 30-second intervals until heated through.

Per serving: Calories: 496; Total dat: 15g; Saturated dat: 5g; Protein: 40g; Total carbs: 49g; Fiber: 4g; Sugar: 2g; Sodium: 412mg

GLUTEN-FREE • NUT-FREE

TURKEY TACO STUFFED BAKED POTATOES

SERVINGS: 4 • **PREP TIME:** 10 minutes • **COOK TIME:** 45 minutes

Tacos are often made with beef but ground turkey is just as good, if not better, with the seasonings of this dish. Turkey is low in calories and an excellent source of protein, potassium, iron, and niacin.

4 sweet potatoes, scrubbed and pricked with a fork

3 teaspoons olive oil, divided

Sea salt

1 pound extra-lean ground turkey

1 tablespoon low-sodium taco seasoning

½ cup salsa

½ cup shredded Mexican cheese

Optional toppings (sliced black olives, avocado, sour cream, corn, black beans, sliced hot peppers)

1. Preheat the oven to 400°F, and line a half baking sheet with parchment paper.

2. Rub the potatoes all over with 1 teaspoon of oil and season with salt. Place them on the baking sheet and bake until they are tender and the skins are golden and crispy, 40 to 45 minutes.

3. While the potatoes are baking, in a large skillet, heat the remaining 2 teaspoons of oil over medium-high heat. Sauté the turkey until cooked through, about 10 minutes. Stir in the taco seasoning, remove from heat, and transfer to a bowl. Let cool completely.

4. Remove the potatoes from the oven and place them in the refrigerator to cool completely.

5. When the potatoes and turkey are cool, cut the potatoes lengthwise to open up a slit in the top, leaving the rest of the skin intact.

6. Spread the potatoes open and use a fork to mash the interior and create a shallow bowl. Evenly distribute the turkey, salsa, cheese, and toppings (if using).

7. Transfer the stuffed potatoes to 4 medium deep meal prep containers, seal, label, and store in the refrigerator for up to 5 days.

REHEATING TIP: To reheat, microwave uncovered for 30-second intervals until heated through.

Per serving: Calories: 329; Total fat: 10g; Saturated fat: 3g; Protein: 32g; Total carbs: 29g; Fiber: 5g; Sugar: 7g; Sodium: 289mg

DAIRY-FREE • GLUTEN-FREE • NUT-FREE

SHAWARMA-RUBBED PORK SHEET-PAN DINNER

SERVINGS: 4 • **PREP TIME:** 15 minutes • **COOK TIME:** 40 minutes

The accompanying vegetables in this dish might remind you of ratatouille—all that's missing is the tomato and eggplant base. The colors of the peppers and zucchini look gorgeous with tender, roasted pork tenderloin. This cut of pork is very lean and will have little fat to trim off, if any. Pork is high in protein and, when combined with the complex carbs from the vegetables, will help you feel full longer.

2 (8-ounce) pork tenderloins, trimmed

2 tablespoons store-bought shawarma spice or homemade Shawarma Spice Blend (page 172)

2 tablespoons olive oil

3 zucchini, cut into 1-inch chunks

2 bell peppers, seeded and cut into 1-inch chunks

1 sweet onion, cut into eighths

3 garlic cloves, thinly sliced

Sea salt

1. Preheat the oven to 400°F. Line a baking sheet with parchment paper.

2. Rub the pork all over with the shawarma spice and place it on one-quarter of the baking sheet.

3. In a large bowl, toss together the oil, zucchini, peppers, onion, and garlic. Season lightly with salt and spread the vegetables on the remaining three-quarters of the baking sheet.

4. Bake the pork and vegetables until the pork is just cooked through and the vegetables are tender, turning the vegetables once halfway through, about 40 minutes.

5. Let the meat rest for 10 minutes, then cut each tenderloin into 4 equal slices.

6. Divide the vegetables into the large side of 4 large (2-compartment) meal prep containers and place two pieces of pork into the smaller side of each container. Place the containers in the refrigerator to cool completely.

7. Seal, label, and store in the refrigerator for up to 5 days.

REHEATING TIP: To reheat, microwave uncovered for 30-second intervals until heated through.

Per serving: Calories: 263; Total Fat: 10g; Saturated Fat: 2g; Protein: 27g; Total Carbs: 17g; Fiber: 3g; Sugar: 8g; Sodium: 181mg

DAIRY-FREE • NUT-FREE

BEEF-STUFFED SQUASH

SERVINGS: 4 • **PREP TIME:** 15 minutes • **COOK TIME:** 40 minutes

This recipe offers your protein, vegetable, and grain side dish all in one attractive package. Squash is technically a fruit, part of the gourd family, but is usually prepared like a vegetable. It is packed with fiber and low in fat.

2 acorn squash, halved and seeded

Nonstick cooking spray

1 cup water

½ cup couscous

1 tablespoon olive oil

1 pound extra-lean ground beef

1 sweet onion, chopped

1 red bell pepper, seeded and chopped

2 teaspoons minced garlic

1 teaspoon ground cumin

Sea salt

Freshly ground black pepper

1. Preheat the oven to 400°F. Line a baking sheet with parchment paper.
2. Grease both the cut sides and the exterior of the squash with cooking spray and place the squash on the baking sheet, cut-side down.
3. Bake the squash for about 40 minutes, until tender but not deflated. Remove from the oven, turn cut-side up and cover with foil to keep warm. Set aside.
4. While the squash is baking, in a small saucepan, bring the water to a boil over high heat. Remove from heat, stir in the couscous, cover, and set aside for 10 minutes.
5. In a large skillet, heat the oil over medium-high heat and brown the beef until cooked through, about 8 minutes. Add the onion, bell pepper, garlic, and cumin and sauté until the vegetables are tender, about 6 minutes.
6. Remove the skillet from the heat and stir in the cooked couscous. Season with salt and pepper.
7. Spoon the beef mixture evenly into each squash half.
8. Place one squash half in each of 4 large deep meal prep containers and place them in the refrigerator to cool.
9. When cool, cover, label, and store in the refrigerator for up to 5 days.

REHEATING TIP: To reheat, microwave uncovered for 30-second intervals until heated through.

Per serving: Calories: 386; Total fat: 10g; Saturated fat: 3g; Protein: 30g; Total carbs: 48g; Fiber: 6g; Sugar: 5g; Sodium: 93mg

DAIRY-FREE • NUT-FREE

SHEET-PAN BEEF FAJITAS

SERVINGS: 4 • **PREP TIME:** 15 minutes • **COOK TIME:** 35 minutes

Fajitas are usually served sizzling on metal platters with a tray of accompaniments such as sour cream, shredded lettuce, cheese, and salsa. This version combines the traditional fajita ingredients on a convenient baking tray.

1 pound sirloin steak

2 tablespoons fajita seasoning, divided

2 tablespoons olive oil, divided

4 bell peppers, any color, seeded and cut into ½-inch slices

1 sweet onion, halved and cut into ½-inch slices

2 teaspoons minced garlic

4 (8-inch) whole-wheat tortillas

½ cup salsa

> **REHEATING TIP:** To reheat, remove the tortilla, and wrap it in a paper towel. Microwave the steak and pepper mixture for 30-second intervals until heated through. Microwave the wrapped tortilla for about 10 seconds.

1. Preheat the oven to 400°F. Line a baking sheet with parchment paper.
2. Season the steak with 1 tablespoon of fajita seasoning.
3. In a large bowl, toss together the remaining 1 tablespoon of fajita seasoning, 1 tablespoon of oil, the peppers, onion, and garlic until coated evenly.
4. Spread the vegetables on two-thirds of the baking sheet and roast in the oven, turning once, about 25 minutes.
5. While the vegetables are roasting, in a large skillet, heat the remaining 1 tablespoon of oil over medium-high heat and pan-sear the steak, turning once, about 5 minutes.
6. Remove the baking sheet from the oven, place the steak on the empty one-third of the baking sheet, and continue roasting for 10 minutes.
7. Remove the baking sheet from the oven. Let the steak rest for 10 minutes, then slice it thinly against the grain.
8. Evenly divide the steak and vegetables into the large sections of 4 large (2-compartment) meal prep containers and place them in the refrigerator to cool.
9. When cool, place a folded tortilla in the small section of each container. Cover, label, and refrigerate for up to 5 days. Evenly divide the salsa into 4 small containers and store with the fajita containers.

Per serving: Calories: 442; Total fat: 16g; Saturated fat: 5g; Protein: 32g; Total carbs: 41g; Fiber: 8g; Sugar: 7g; Sodium: 623mg

CHAPTER 15

Snacks and Sweets

Avocado Cherry Kale Smoothie 160

Green Chia Smoothie 161

Mocha Protein Smoothie 162

Pomegranate Blueberry Smoothie 163

Chickpea Salad Pinwheels 164

Golden Roasted Chickpeas 165

Chocolate Sesame Oat Bites 166

Coconut Maple Truffles 167

Orange Pots de Crème 168

Peanut Butter Honey Fruit Wrap 169

Southwest Broccoli Salad, page 147

GLUTEN-FREE • NUT-FREE • VEGETARIAN

AVOCADO CHERRY KALE SMOOTHIE

SERVINGS: 5 • **PREP TIME:** 10 minutes, plus 1 hour to freeze

You should be a cherry lover to partake in this thick, creamy smoothie because that lush fruit provides the prominent flavor. Cherries can be expensive off-season, so frozen is a good option if it isn't May through September. Frozen cherries are also pitted, so your prep time is cut down. Cherries are an excellent source of antioxidants as well as vitamins B, C, and E.

- 2 avocados, diced into 1-inch chunks
- 3 cups fresh kale
- 1 (16-ounce) bag frozen, unsweetened cherries
- 1 (half-gallon) container 2 percent milk or vanilla almond milk
- 5 tablespoons honey

1. Spread the avocados and kale on a parchment-lined baking sheet, keeping them separated, and place in the freezer until frozen, about 1 hour.

2. Evenly divide the frozen avocado and kale into 5 medium sealable bags. Add the cherries, dividing them evenly as well. Press out the air, seal the bags, and label them. Place them in the freezer for up to 1 month.

3. Evenly divide the milk and honey among 5 medium meal prep containers or jars, about 1⅔ cups of milk and 1 tablespoon of honey in each. Seal, label, and refrigerate for up to 1 week.

4. Combine 1 portion of solid ingredients and 1 portion of liquid ingredients in a blender and blend until smooth. Add a little water if the texture is too thick.

Per serving: Calories: 400; Total fat: 16g; Saturated fat: 5g; Protein: 15g; Total carbs: 55g; Fiber: 9g; Sugar: 46g; Sodium: 158mg

DAIRY-FREE • GLUTEN-FREE • NUT-FREE • VEGAN

GREEN CHIA SMOOTHIE

SERVINGS: 5 • **PREP TIME:** 10 minutes, plus 1 hour to freeze

Chia seeds provide both texture and a significant nutrition boost to this sweet smoothie. If you want an even thicker texture, combine the seeds with the orange juice a couple of hours before whipping up the smoothie. The orange juice, mango, and banana create a tropical flavor reminiscent of a fruit cocktail. Add a festive umbrella and enjoy the drink on a sunny patio to complete the theme.

5 bananas, cut into 1-inch chunks

5 cups fresh baby spinach

1 (12-ounce) bag frozen unsweetened mango

5 cups orange juice

5 tablespoons chia seeds

1. Spread the bananas and spinach on a parchment-lined baking sheet, keeping them separated, and place in the freezer until frozen, about 1 hour.

2. Evenly divide the frozen bananas and spinach into 5 medium sealable bags. Add the mango, dividing it evenly as well. Press out the air, seal the bags, and label them. Place them in the freezer for up to 1 month.

3. Evenly divide the orange juice and chia seeds among 5 medium meal prep containers or jars. Seal, label, and refrigerate for up to 1 week.

4. Combine 1 portion of the solid ingredients and 1 portion of the orange juice and chia seeds in a blender and blend until smooth. Add a little water if the texture is too thick.

Per serving: Calories: 344; Total fat: 5g; Saturated fat: 1g; Protein: 7g; Total carbs: 72g; Fiber: 10g; Sugar: 44g; Sodium: 33mg

GLUTEN-FREE • VEGETARIAN

MOCHA PROTEIN SMOOTHIE

SERVINGS: 5 • **PREP TIME:** 10 minutes, plus 2 hours to freeze

Coffee might seem like an unusual ingredient in a smoothie, but when combined with sweet bananas and rich chocolate protein powder, it becomes an energy-packed snack. Freezing the coffee ensures a milkshake-like texture. Look for a protein powder that is low in sugar to ensure this snack is not too high in calories. For extra chocolatey flavor, add half a teaspoon of cocoa powder per portion.

20 ounces brewed coffee

5 bananas, cut into 1-inch chunks

2 cups sweetened vanilla almond milk

2½ cups plain Greek yogurt

5 scoops chocolate protein powder

1. Pour the coffee into 2 ice cube trays and place in the freezer to freeze solid, about 2 hours.

2. Spread the banana pieces on a half baking sheet and place in the freezer until frozen, about 1 hour.

3. Evenly divide the frozen banana pieces among 5 medium sealable bags and add 4 frozen coffee cubes to each bag. Press out the air, seal the bags, and label them. Place them in the freezer for up to 1 month.

4. Evenly divide the almond milk, yogurt, and protein powder among 5 medium meal prep containers. Seal, label, and refrigerate for up to 1 week.

5. To serve, take one portion of coffee and banana pieces out of the freezer and place in a blender along with 1 portion of the milk, yogurt, and protein powder. Blend until smooth and serve immediately.

Per serving: Calories: 391; Total fat: 8g; Saturated fat:3 g; Protein: 30g; Total carbs: 51g; Fiber: 7g; Sugar: 36g; Sodium: 342mg

DAIRY-FREE • GLUTEN-FREE • NUT-FREE • VEGAN

POMEGRANATE BLUEBERRY SMOOTHIE

SERVINGS: 5 • **PREP TIME:** 10 minutes, plus 2 hours to freeze

Pomegranate can be a difficult fruit to prepare, so using just the juice saves time. The tangy, distinctive flavor of the juice is perfect with the earthy kale and sweet maple syrup in this smoothie. Pomegranate is higher in antioxidants than most fruits, including the blueberries in this recipe, and it is also a wonderful source of vitamins C and K.

15 ounces pomegranate juice

5 cups fresh kale

1 (12-ounce) bag frozen blueberries

1 cup unsweetened apple juice

1 cup water

5 tablespoons maple syrup

1. Pour the pomegranate juice into an ice cube tray and place in the freezer to freeze solid, about 2 hours.

2. Spread the kale on a baking sheet and place in the freezer until frozen, about 1 hour.

3. Evenly divide the frozen kale and blueberries among 5 medium sealable bags. Add 3 pomegranate juice cubes to each bag. Press out the air, seal the bags, and label them. Place them in the freezer for up to 1 month.

4. Evenly divide the apple juice, water, and maple syrup among 5 medium meal prep containers. Seal, label, and refrigerate for up to 1 week.

5. To serve, take one portion of pomegranate juice and kale out of the freezer and place it in a blender along with 1 portion of the liquid ingredients. Blend until smooth and serve immediately.

Per serving: Calories: 163; Total fat: 1g; Saturated fat: 0g; Protein: 1g; Total carbs: 39g; Fiber: 3g; Sugar: 33g; Sodium: 19mg

DAIRY-FREE • NUT-FREE • VEGETARIAN

CHICKPEA SALAD PINWHEELS

SERVINGS: 4 • **PREP TIME:** 25 minutes

Mock "egg" salad is a staple meal in vegan cuisine, and it is often made with chickpeas or raw soaked cashews. This version uses chickpeas along with standard egg salad ingredients such as mayonnaise and lemon juice. Add some chopped celery and dill pickle for a bit of crunch and flavor. The benefit of this tempting chickpea salad over egg salad is that the legume version keeps better for a meal prep menu and will not make the tortilla soggy.

1 (16-ounce) can low-sodium chickpeas, drained and rinsed

Juice of ½ lemon

2 tablespoons mayonnaise

Sea salt

Freshly ground black pepper

4 (8-inch) multigrain tortillas

1½ cups shredded carrot

1. In a small bowl, use a potato masher to mash the chickpeas, lemon juice, and mayonnaise until a spreadable paste forms. Season with salt and pepper.
2. Lay the tortillas on a clean work surface and evenly spread the chickpea mixture over each of them, leaving a 1-inch border along the edge. Top the chickpea mixture evenly with the carrot.
3. Roll up the tortillas tightly and wrap each in plastic wrap. Refrigerate for up to 5 days.
4. To serve, trim off the empty tortilla ends. Cut each tortilla carefully into six round pieces.

Per serving: Calories: 327; Total fat: 11g; Saturated fat: 3g; Protein: 12g; Total carbs: 45g; Fiber: 11g; Sugar: 7g; Sodium: 243mg

DAIRY-FREE • GLUTEN-FREE • NUT-FREE • VEGAN

GOLDEN ROASTED CHICKPEAS

SERVINGS: 5 • **PREP TIME:** 10 minutes • **COOK TIME:** 35 minutes

Roasted chickpeas are a trendy snack right up there with kale chips, which have shown up in most grocery stores in the organic aisle. If you purchase the premade chickpea snack, it can be expensive and there will be lots of additives you might not want to eat. Homemade crispy chickpeas avoid these unhealthy embellishments and provide all the benefits of these legumes such as fiber, protein, and healthy fats.

2 (16-ounce) cans low-sodium chickpeas, drained and rinsed

1 tablespoon olive oil

½ teaspoon garlic powder

½ teaspoon ground cumin

Sea salt

1. Dry the chickpeas completely using paper towels or a clean kitchen cloth.
2. Preheat the oven to 375°F. Line a baking sheet with parchment paper.
3. In a large bowl, toss together the dried chickpeas, oil, garlic powder, and cumin until coated evenly.
4. Transfer the chickpeas to the baking sheet and spread them out in a single layer.
5. Bake the chickpeas until golden and crisp, about 35 minutes.
6. Remove the chickpeas from the oven and season lightly with salt.
7. Allow the chickpeas to cool completely on the baking sheet. Divide them evenly among 5 medium sealable plastic bags, press out the air, and store at room temperature for up to 5 days.

SUBSTITUTION TIP: Try an assortment of seasonings with these crispy treats, such as chili powder, coriander, curry, paprika, turmeric, cinnamon, or cloves, to create fabulous combinations.

Per serving: Calories: 187; Total fat: 5g; Saturated fat: 1g; Protein: 9g; Total carbs: 27g; Fiber: 8g; Sugar: 5g; Sodium: 22mg

DAIRY-FREE • GLUTEN-FREE • VEGAN

CHOCOLATE SESAME OAT BITES

SERVINGS: 10 • **PREP TIME:** 15 minutes, plus 30 minutes to chill • **COOK TIME:** 6 minutes

You will be reminded of a popular chocolate and peanut butter candy bar when you bite into these delectable treats. The hint of sesame and the texture from the oats just makes this homemade snack even better. This recipe uses cocoa powder for the chocolate flavor, and a little goes a long way. Cocoa is not just a dessert ingredient—historically, it was a folk remedy used for various ailments, and it is thought to reduce the risk of cardiovascular disease and type 2 diabetes.

½ **cup peanut butter**

¼ **cup brown sugar**

1 tablespoon cocoa powder

1 cup rolled oats

2 tablespoons sesame seeds

1. Line a baking sheet with parchment paper.
2. In a medium saucepan, stir together the peanut butter, brown sugar, and cocoa. Place the saucepan over medium heat and stir constantly until the sugar is dissolved and the mixture is simmering slightly, about 6 minutes.
3. Remove from heat and stir in the oats and sesame seeds until well combined.
4. Using a tablespoon or a cookie dough scoop, portion out 20 equal pieces of the mixture and place on the baking sheet.
5. Refrigerate until firm, about 30 minutes.
6. Place two bites each into 10 small sealable plastic bags, seal, and store in the freezer for up to 1 month. To serve, thaw at room temperature for about 15 minutes.

Per serving: Calories: 163; Total fat: 9g; Saturated fat: 2g; Protein: 6g; Total carbs: 17g; Fiber: 3g; Sugar: 5g; Sodium: 57mg

DAIRY-FREE • GLUTEN-FREE • NUT-FREE • VEGAN

COCONUT MAPLE TRUFFLES

SERVINGS: 5 • **PREP TIME:** 15 minutes

These are not actually truffles—there is no chocolate or ganache here—but the general shape is so similar that to call them truffles seemed apt. The addition of both dates and maple syrup might make you assume the taste will be cloyingly sweet, but neutral oats, warm cinnamon, and unsweetened coconut balance out the flavors very well. If you prefer less sweetness, reduce the maple syrup by half, but don't cut the dates because they are required to create "dough" that sticks together.

1 cup rolled oats

4 Medjool dates

¼ cup maple syrup

¼ teaspoon ground cinnamon

½ cup unsweetened shredded coconut

1. Place the oats, dates, maple syrup, and cinnamon in a food processor and pulse until the mixture holds together.

2. Place the shredded coconut on a plate.

3. Roll the oat mixture into about 15 balls, then roll the balls in the coconut.

4. Place 3 balls each in 5 medium sealable plastic bags, press out the air, and seal. Store the truffles in the freezer for up to 1 month. To serve, thaw at room temperature for about 15 minutes.

Per serving: Calories: 244; Total fat: 5g; Saturated fat: 3g; Protein: 6g; Total carbs: 46g; Fiber: 5g; Sugar: 23g; Sodium: 6mg

GLUTEN-FREE • NUT-FREE • VEGETARIAN

ORANGE POTS DE CRÈME

SERVINGS: 5 • **PREP TIME:** 10 minutes • **COOK TIME:** 16 minutes

Pots de crème is a fancy way of saying pudding, and this pudding has a luscious, velvety texture that melts in the mouth. Orange and cream are a common pairing, so the flavor might seem familiar. To turn these simple creations into a high-end dessert, add a scoop of whipped cream or top with chocolate shavings.

6 large egg yolks
2 cups half-and-half
Juice and zest of 1 large orange
¼ cup granulated sugar
2 teaspoons pure vanilla extract
Pinch sea salt

1. In a medium bowl, whisk the egg yolks until smooth. Set aside.
2. In a medium saucepan over medium-low heat, stir together the half-and-half, orange juice, orange zest, sugar, vanilla, and salt until well mixed. Stir constantly until it just comes to a simmer, about 6 minutes.
3. Slowly pour the mixture into the bowl with the egg yolks, whisking constantly.
4. Transfer the egg mixture back to the saucepan and reduce the heat to low.
5. Cook, whisking constantly, until the mixture thickens and coats the back of a spoon, about 10 minutes.
6. Remove from heat and evenly divide the custard into 5 medium containers.
7. Chill the custard with plastic wrap pressed on the surface until set and cold, about 2 hours.
8. Seal the containers and store them in the refrigerator for up to 5 days.

Per serving: Calories: 243; Total fat: 17g; Saturated fat: 9g; Protein: 6g; Total carbs: 17g; Fiber: 0g; Sugar: 16g; Sodium: 50mg

DAIRY-FREE • VEGETARIAN

PEANUT BUTTER HONEY FRUIT WRAP

SERVINGS: 5 • **PREP TIME:** 15 minutes

This snack is a version of a classic childhood sandwich featuring peanut butter, banana, and honey. The addition of fiber-rich oats and a whole-wheat tortilla creates a more grown-up version of the dish. Make sure the bananas are ripe but not mushy so that they last the week in the refrigerator. Try crunchy peanut butter instead of smooth for a lovely texture and strong peanut taste.

5 (6-inch) whole-wheat tortillas

7½ tablespoons smooth or crunchy peanut butter

2 bananas, thinly sliced

¼ cup rolled oats

2 tablespoons honey

1. Lay the tortillas on a clean work surface and spread 1½ tablespoons of peanut butter onto each tortilla, leaving ½ inch around the edges.

2. Evenly divide the banana slices among the tortillas, placing the fruit on the side closest to you and leaving about 1½ inches on either side.

3. Sprinkle the oats evenly over the banana and drizzle evenly with honey.

4. Fold the left and right edges of the tortillas into the center, laying the edges over the banana. Taking the tortilla edge closest to you, fold it over the fruit and side pieces. Roll the tortillas away from you, creating a snug wrap.

5. Wrap the tortillas tightly in plastic wrap and store in the refrigerator for up to 5 days.

SUBSTITUTION TIP: Blueberries or sliced apples, strawberries, peaches, or mango can be used in place of the banana for a delicious snack. Omit the honey if you enjoy a more assertive peanut taste.

Per serving: Calories: 369; Total fat: 17g; Saturated fat: 5g; Protein: 11g; Total carbs: 47g; Fiber: 7g; Sugar: 16g; Sodium: 276mg

CHAPTER 16

Seasonings, Dressings, and Sauces

Shawarma Spice Blend 172

All-Purpose Spice Rub 173

Simple Herbed Balsamic Dressing 174

Hoisin Dressing and Marinade 175

Creamy Peanut Dressing 176

Traditional Basil Pesto 177

Tzatziki Sauce 178

Pico de Gallo 179

Shawarma-Rubbed Pork Sheet-Pan Dinner, page 155

DAIRY-FREE • GLUTEN-FREE • NUT-FREE • VEGAN

SHAWARMA SPICE BLEND

MAKES: ½ cup • **PREP TIME:** 5 minutes

Shawarma might be familiar to you since this spice blend is used in many popular street foods. The spice blend is associated with proteins such as chicken and is also delicious with vegetables and fish and as a topping for bread and dips. Try a little sprinkle in a soup or stew to perk up the flavor and give the dish a Middle Eastern flair.

- 2½ **tablespoons garlic powder**
- 1½ **tablespoons ground allspice**
- 1 **tablespoon ground cardamom**
- 1 **tablespoon ground cinnamon**
- 1½ **teaspoons freshly ground black pepper**
- 1½ teaspoons chili powder
- 1 teaspoon sea salt

1. In a small bowl, stir together the garlic powder, allspice, cardamom, cinnamon, pepper, chili powder, and salt until well blended.

2. Transfer the spice blend to a container or jar with a lid and store in a cool, dry place for up to 1 month.

Per serving (1 teaspoon): Calories: 7; Total fat: 0g; Saturated fat: 0g; Protein: 0g; Total carbs: 1g; Fiber: 0g; Sugar: 0g; Sodium: 103mg

DAIRY-FREE • GLUTEN-FREE • NUT-FREE • VEGAN

ALL-PURPOSE SPICE RUB

MAKES: ½ cup • **PREP TIME:** 5 minutes

Spices are one of the best ways to flavor your recipes without adding too much sodium or having to fuss with complicated ingredients. A sprinkle of spices on a salad or vegetables can elevate them, and a spice rub on a protein is all that is required for a satisfying meal. Having an all-purpose spice rub in your pantry means you don't have to completely fill your spice drawer with expensive products.

2 tablespoons garlic powder

1 tablespoon dried basil

1 tablespoon dried oregano

1 tablespoon celery salt

2 teaspoons dried thyme

1 teaspoon freshly ground black pepper

1. In a small bowl, stir together the garlic powder, basil, oregano, celery salt, thyme, and pepper until well blended.

2. Transfer the spice blend to a container or jar with a lid and store in a cool, dry place for up to 1 month.

Per serving (1 teaspoon): Calories: 6; Total fat: 0g; Saturated fat: 0g; Protein: 0g; Total carbs: 1g; Fiber: 0g; Sugar: 0g; Sodium: 2mg

DAIRY-FREE • GLUTEN-FREE • NUT-FREE • VEGAN

SIMPLE HERBED BALSAMIC DRESSING

MAKES: 1 cup • **PREP TIME:** 10 minutes

If you have been cooking for a while or enjoy reading about culinary terms or techniques, an emulsion should be familiar to you. Dressings and vinaigrettes are usually emulsions, which means that two unmixable ingredients, like oil and vinegar, are held together by a process, like whisking, or an ingredient, such as the mustard in this recipe. You will have to emulsify this dressing again before using it by shaking the container or whisking again.

½ cup olive oil

3 tablespoons balsamic vinegar

1 teaspoon Dijon mustard

2 tablespoons chopped fresh basil

1 tablespoon chopped fresh thyme

1 teaspoon chopped fresh oregano

Sea salt

Freshly ground black pepper

1. In a small bowl, whisk together the oil, vinegar, mustard, basil, thyme, and oregano until blended.
2. Season with salt and pepper.
3. Store the dressing in a container or jar with a lid in the refrigerator for up to 2 weeks. Shake well each time before using.

COOKING TIP: Instead of using a bowl to combine the ingredients, add everything to a mason jar, shake to combine, and store in the same jar. Double this dressing because it will become a staple in your recipes.

Per serving (2 tablespoons): Calories: 126; Total fat: 13g; Saturated fat: 2g; Protein: 0g; Total carbs: 1g; Fiber: 0g; Sugar: 1g; Sodium: 17mg

DAIRY-FREE • NUT-FREE • VEGAN

HOISIN DRESSING and MARINADE

MAKES: ⅔ cup • **PREP TIME:** 10 minutes

Many dressings are Mediterranean-based, with lots of fresh herbs, vinegar, and olive oil. This dressing has a rich flavor due to the addition of sesame oil, soy sauce, and ginger along with the distinctive hoisin sauce. For a simple meal, toss a couple of tablespoons of this dressing with cooked rice noodles and store-bought broccoli slaw and serve it cold. Delicious!

⅓ **cup hoisin sauce**

2 tablespoons brown sugar

1 tablespoon low-sodium soy sauce

1 tablespoon peeled grated fresh ginger

2 teaspoons sesame oil

2 teaspoons minced garlic

1. In a small bowl, whisk together the hoisin sauce, brown sugar, soy sauce, ginger, sesame oil, and garlic until blended.

2. Store the dressing in a container or jar with a lid in the refrigerator for up to 2 weeks. Shake well each time before using.

Per serving (2 tablespoons): Calories: 59; Total fat: 2g; Saturated fat: 0g; Protein: 1g; Total carbs: 10g; Fiber: 0g; Sugar: 7g; Sodium: 299mg

DAIRY-FREE • VEGAN

CREAMY PEANUT DRESSING

MAKES: ¾ cup • **PREP TIME:** 10 minutes

Peanut sauce is used in many countries like ketchup is used in North America. It is a dip, topping, sauce, and condiment. Peanut sauce can also be tossed with noodles and vegetables to create incredibly flavorful side dishes and main courses. If possible, do not leave out the red pepper flakes because the subtle layer of heat enhances the other ingredients. Try this sauce with chicken kebabs and a bowl of fluffy rice.

½ cup smooth peanut butter

3 tablespoons low-sodium soy sauce

Juice of 1 lime

2 tablespoons maple syrup

2 teaspoons minced garlic

Pinch red pepper flakes (optional)

1. In a small bowl, whisk together the peanut butter, soy sauce, lime juice, maple syrup, garlic, and red pepper flakes (if using) until blended.
2. Store the dressing in a container or jar with a lid in the refrigerator for up to 1 week. Thin with water if necessary and shake well each time before using.

SUBSTITUTION TIP: Any nut butter or seed butter tastes delicious in this spicy sauce. Soy butter products are a good choice if you have a nut allergy but still want to enjoy these complex flavors.

Per serving (2 tablespoons): Calories: 149; Total fat: 8g; Saturated fat: 1g; Protein: 7g; Total carbs: 14g; Fiber: 1g; Sugar: 6g; Sodium: 312mg

GLUTEN-FREE • VEGETARIAN

TRADITIONAL BASIL PESTO

MAKES: 1 cup • **PREP TIME:** 10 minutes

Knowing how to make a basic pesto like this one is a culinary necessity. Pesto is one of those condiments that you should always keep on hand because it can be used in almost any type of dish except desserts. Fresh basil can be a difficult ingredient to find in some markets, but this herb is extremely easy to grow in a garden or windowsill pot. Simply snip off the leaves required for the recipe and let the plant grow.

1½ cups packed fresh basil leaves

¼ cup pine nuts

2 tablespoons grated Parmesan cheese

2 teaspoons minced garlic

¼ cup olive oil

Sea salt

Freshly ground black pepper

1. Place the basil, pine nuts, cheese, and garlic in a blender or food processor and pulse until the ingredients are finely chopped, scraping down the sides with a spatula at least once.

2. Add the oil and pulse until incorporated and a thick paste forms. Season with salt and pepper.

3. Transfer to a sealed container and store in the refrigerator for up to 1 week.

Per serving (2 tablespoons): Calories: 95; Total fat: 10g; Saturated fat: 1g; Protein: 1g; Total carbs: 1g; Fiber: 0g; Sugar: 0g; Sodium: 42mg

GLUTEN-FREE • NUT-FREE • **VEGETARIAN**

TZATZIKI SAUCE

MAKES: 1½ cups • **PREP TIME:** 10 minutes

Tzatziki is a versatile sauce, creamy, fresh-tasting, and redolent with fresh dill and garlic. You can use this sauce on almost any type of protein, including beef, fish, and tofu, or as a topping on wraps, sandwiches, dips, and soups. Lime juice can be used in place of the vinegar with lovely results if you like an even tangier flavor. This sauce holds up very well, so it is ideal for meal prep menus.

1 cup plain Greek yogurt

½ large English cucumber, grated, with all the liquid squeezed out

1½ tablespoons chopped fresh dill

1 tablespoon olive oil

2 teaspoons apple cider vinegar

1 teaspoon minced garlic

Sea salt

1. In a small bowl, stir together the yogurt, cucumber, dill, oil, vinegar, and garlic until well blended. Season with salt.

2. Transfer the sauce to a sealed container and store in the refrigerator for up to 4 days.

Per serving (¼ cup): Calories: 55; Total fat: 4g; Saturated fat: 1g; Protein: 2g; Total carbs: 4g; Fiber: 1g; Sugar: 2g; Sodium: 46mg

DAIRY-FREE • GLUTEN-FREE • NUT-FREE • VEGAN

PICO DE GALLO

MAKES: 2 cups • **PREP TIME:** 15 minutes

Pico de gallo, also known as "salsa fresca" or "salsa cruda," is a fresh salsa made with tomatoes, onion, and lime juice. It can include hot peppers, depending on your preference. This recipe does include an entire jalapeño pepper with the seeds, so it has some heat. The substance that gives the heat is called capsaicin, and it also provides some medicinal benefits. Capsaicin can support weight loss, reduce the risk of heart disease, and help manage pain associated with arthritis. If you don't like heat, reduce the amount of the jalapeño pepper used or scrape out the seeds before chopping it.

1 pound tomatoes, seeded and chopped

1 jalapeño pepper, chopped

¼ red onion, chopped

Juice and zest of 1 lime

2 tablespoons chopped fresh cilantro

Sea salt

Freshly ground black pepper

1. In a medium bowl, stir together the tomatoes, jalapeño pepper, onion, lime juice, lime zest, and cilantro until well mixed. Season with salt and black pepper.

2. Transfer the mixture to a sealed container and store in the refrigerator for up to 4 days.

Per serving (2 tablespoons): Calories: 7; Total fat: 0g; Saturated fat: 0g; Protein: 0g; Total carbs: 2g; Fiber: 0g; Sugar: 1g; Sodium: 11mg

Measurement Conversions

VOLUME EQUIVALENTS (LIQUID)

US Standard	US Standard (ounces)	Metric (approximate)
2 tablespoons	1 fl. oz.	30 mL
¼ cup	2 fl. oz.	60 mL
½ cup	4 fl. oz.	120 mL
1 cup	8 fl. oz.	240 mL
1½ cups	12 fl. oz.	355 mL
2 cups or 1 pint	16 fl. oz.	475 mL
4 cups or 1 quart	32 fl. oz.	1 L
1 gallon	128 fl. oz.	4 L

OVEN TEMPERATURES

Fahrenheit (F)	Celsius (C) (approximate)
250°F	120°C
300°F	150°C
325°F	165°C
350°F	180°C
375°F	190°C
400°F	200°C
425°F	220°C
450°F	230°C

VOLUME EQUIVALENTS (DRY)

US Standard	Metric (approximate)
⅛ teaspoon	0.5 mL
¼ teaspoon	1 mL
½ teaspoon	2 mL
¾ teaspoon	4 mL
1 teaspoon	5 mL
1 tablespoon	15 mL
¼ cup	59 mL
⅓ cup	79 mL
½ cup	118 mL
⅔ cup	156 mL
¾ cup	177 mL
1 cup	235 mL
2 cups or 1 pint	475 mL
3 cups	700 mL
4 cups or 1 quart	1 L

WEIGHT EQUIVALENTS

US Standard	Metric (approximate)
½ ounce	15 g
1 ounce	30 g
2 ounces	60 g
4 ounces	115 g
8 ounces	225 g
12 ounces	340 g
16 ounces or 1 pound	455 g

Index

A

All-Purpose Spice Rub, 173
Almond Quinoa Pudding, 69
Antipasto Couscous Salad, 116
Apple Pie Overnight Oats, 25
Artichoke hearts
   Antipasto Couscous
      Salad, 116
Asparagus
   Pesto Tilapia Vegetable
      Packets, 58
Avocado Cherry Kale
   Smoothie, 160

B

Bacon
   Bacon Breakfast Cassoulet, 45
   Brussels Sprout Egg
      Skillet, 143
Baked Lemon Garlic Trout
   with Potato Wedges, 97
Balsamic-Marinated Halibut
   with Farro, 152
Bananas
   Banana Baked Oatmeal, 65
   Banana Walnut Couscous, 136
   Green Chia Smoothie, 161
   Mocha Protein Smoothie, 162
   Peanut Butter Honey
      Fruit Wrap, 169
Beans
   Bacon Breakfast Cassoulet, 45
   Black Bean Chili
      Quesadillas, 46
   Mediterranean
      Layered Dip, 49
   Slow Cooker Chipotle
      Chili, 128
   Southwest Broccoli Salad, 147
   Spicy Vegetarian Chili, 17
   White Bean Breakfast
      Burritos, 125
Beef
   Beef-Stuffed Squash, 156
   Korean-Style Beef with
      Brown Rice, 107
   Marinated Flank Steak
      with Pico de Gallo, 38
   Sheet-Pan Beef Fajitas, 157
   Slow Cooker Tomato
      and Beef Stew, 47
   Spaghetti Bolognese, 27
Beet and Berry Smoothie, 119
Berries
   Beet and Berry Smoothie, 119
   Crêpes with Raspberries, 85
   Fluffy Buttermilk Pancakes, 35
   Granola Muesli, 95
   Lemon Mascarpone
      Cream Sauce with
      Strawberries, 39
   Pomegranate Blueberry
      Smoothie, 163
   Strawberry French Toast
      Casserole, 115
   Wheat Berry Harvest Salad, 76
Bisphenol A (BPA), 5
Black Bean Chili Quesadillas, 46
Bok choy
   Hoisin Salmon with
      Bok Choy, 151
   Korean-Style Beef with
      Brown Rice, 107
Bowls
   Mediterranean Turkey
      Bowls, 66
   Noodle Bowls with
      Peanut Sauce, 149
   Salad Bowls with Tzatziki
      Sauce, 106
   Savory Farro Breakfast
      Bowl, 140
Broccoli
   Cheesy Chicken Broccoli
      Casserole, 18
   Garam Masala Chicken
      Thighs with Broccoli, 57
   Pesto Tilapia Vegetable
      Packets, 58
   Savory Farro Breakfast
      Bowl, 140
   Southwest Broccoli Salad, 147
Brussels Sprout Egg Skillet, 143
Bulgur
   Sweet Potato Tabbouleh, 146
Buttermilk Pancakes, Fluffy, 35

C

Cabbage. *See also* Coleslaw
   Oktoberfest Soup, 117
Canadian Bacon and Goat
   Cheese Egg Muffins, 142
Carrots
   Brussels Sprout Egg
      Skillet, 143
   Chicken Spinach
      Chowder, 126
   Chickpea Salad
      Pinwheels, 164
   Oktoberfest Soup, 117
   Sesame Zoodles with
      Summer Vegetables, 36
   Sheet-Pan Chicken
      Parmesan, 78
   Simple Slow Cooker
      Chicken Stew, 87
   Slow Cooker Tomato
      and Beef Stew, 47
   Spice-Rubbed Pork
      Tenderloin, 48

Split Pea Root Vegetable
     Soup, 67
Veggie and Feta Egg
     Sandwich, 135
Cashew-Crusted Halibut
     with Brown Rice, 88
Celeriac
  Shawarma Chicken with
     Root Vegetables, 37
Celery
  Chicken Spinach
     Chowder, 126
  Simple Slow Cooker
     Chicken Stew, 87
  Split Pea Root Vegetable
     Soup, 67
Cereal
  Sesame Brown Rice Treats, 59
  Spicy Snack Mix, 29
Cheese
  Black Bean Chili
     Quesadillas, 46
  Canadian Bacon and Goat
     Cheese Egg Muffins, 142
  Cheesy Chicken Broccoli
     Casserole, 18
  Chicken Caprese Salad, 148
  Chicken Cobb Salad, 26
  Chicken Pesto Penne, 153
  Ham and Cheese Breakfast
     Casserole, 141
  Mediterranean Breakfast
     Wraps, 75
  Mediterranean
     Layered Dip, 49
  Mediterranean Turkey
     Bowls, 66
  Savory Farro Breakfast
     Bowl, 140
  Sheet-Pan Chicken
     Parmesan, 78
  Spaghetti Bolognese, 27
  Spinach Mac and Cheese, 86
  Sweet Potato Spinach
     Frittata, 105

Traditional Basil Pesto, 177
Turkey Taco Stuffed
     Baked Potatoes, 154
Veggie and Feta Egg
     Sandwich, 135
White Bean Breakfast
     Burritos, 125
Cheesy Chicken Broccoli
     Casserole, 18
Cherry Avocado Kale
     Smoothie, 160
Chia Smoothie, Green, 161
Chicken
  Cheesy Chicken Broccoli
     Casserole, 18
  Chicken Caprese Salad, 148
  Chicken Cobb Salad, 26
  Chicken Pesto Penne, 153
  Chicken Spinach
     Chowder, 126
  Creamy Curry Chicken
     and Rice, 98
  Garam Masala Chicken
     Thighs with Broccoli, 57
  Paprika Chicken with
     Butter Noodles, 108
  Salad Bowls with Tzatziki
     Sauce, 106
  Shawarma Chicken with
     Root Vegetables, 37
  Sheet-Pan Chicken
     Parmesan, 78
  Simple Slow Cooker
     Chicken Stew, 87
Chickpeas
  Chickpea Root Vegetable
     Curry, 150
  Chickpea Salad
     Pinwheels, 164
  Classic Hummus, 89
  Golden Roasted
     Chickpeas, 165
  Salad Bowls with Tzatziki
     Sauce, 106

Chilis
  Slow Cooker Chipotle
     Chili, 128
  Spicy Vegetarian Chili, 17
Chocolate
  Chocolate Cashew Bars, 19
  Chocolate Hazelnut
     Steel-Cut Oats, 134
  Chocolate Mint Mousse, 129
  Chocolate Sesame
     Oat Bites, 166
  Mocha Protein Smoothie, 162
Classic Hummus, 89
Coconut
  Coconut Maple Truffles, 167
  Quinoa Pecan Granola, 137
Coconut milk
  Creamy Curry Chicken
     and Rice, 98
Coffee
  Mocha Protein Smoothie, 162
Coleslaw
  Crunchy Lettuce Cajun
     Coleslaw Wraps, 16
  Noodle Bowls with
     Peanut Sauce, 149
Corn
  Black Bean Chili
     Quesadillas, 46
  Chicken Spinach
     Chowder, 126
  Southwest Broccoli Salad, 147
  Veggie and Feta Egg
     Sandwich, 135
Couscous
  Antipasto Couscous
     Salad, 116
  Banana Walnut Couscous, 136
  Beef-Stuffed Squash, 156
  Creamy Curry Chicken
     and Rice, 98
Creamy Peanut Dressing, 176
Creamy Potato Leek Soup, 56
Crêpes with Raspberries, 85
Crispy Chili Kale Chips, 99

INDEX   183

Crunchy Lettuce Cajun Coleslaw Wraps, 16
Cucumbers
　Salad Bowls with Tzatziki Sauce, 106
　Tzatziki Sauce, 178

D

Dairy-free
　All-Purpose Spice Rub, 173
　Almond Quinoa Pudding, 69
　Antipasto Couscous Salad, 116
　Bacon Breakfast Cassoulet, 45
　Baked Lemon Garlic Trout with Potato Wedges, 97
　Balsamic-Marinated Halibut with Farro, 152
　Banana Baked Oatmeal, 65
　Beef-Stuffed Squash, 156
　Beet and Berry Smoothie, 119
　Brussels Sprout Egg Skillet, 143
　Cashew-Crusted Halibut with Brown Rice, 88
　Chickpea Root Vegetable Curry, 150
　Chickpea Salad Pinwheels, 164
　Chocolate Sesame Oat Bites, 166
　Classic Hummus, 89
　Coconut Maple Truffles, 167
　Creamy Curry Chicken and Rice, 98
　Creamy Peanut Dressing, 176
　Crispy Chili Kale Chips, 99
　Garam Masala Chicken Thighs with Broccoli, 57
　Golden Roasted Chickpeas, 165
　Green Chia Smoothie, 161
　Hoisin Dressing and Marinade, 175
　Hoisin Salmon with Bok Choy, 151
　Honey Sesame Salmon with Squash, 68
　Korean-Style Beef with Brown Rice, 107
　Marinated Flank Steak with Pico de Gallo, 38
　Noodle Bowls with Peanut Sauce, 149
　Oktoberfest Soup, 117
　Peanut Butter Honey Fruit Wrap, 169
　Pico de Gallo, 179
　Pomegranate Blueberry Smoothie, 163
　Pumpkin Sausage Egg Casserole, 55
　Quinoa Pecan Granola, 137
　Roasted Tofu Acorn Squash Bake, 127
　Salmon, Potato, and French Bean Sheet-Pan Bake, 28
　Sesame Zoodles with Summer Vegetables, 36
　Shawarma Chicken with Root Vegetables, 37
　Shawarma-Rubbed Pork Sheet-Pan Dinner, 155
　Shawarma Spice Blend, 172
　Sheet-Pan Beef Fajitas, 157
　Sheet-Pan Country Breakfast, 139
　Sheet-Pan Sausage and Peppers, 96
　Simple Herbed Balsamic Dressing, 174
　Simple Slow Cooker Chicken Stew, 87
　Slow Cooker Chipotle Chili, 128
　Slow Cooker Tomato and Beef Stew, 47
　Spice-Rubbed Pork Tenderloin, 48
　Spicy Snack Mix, 29
　Spicy Vegetarian Chili, 17
　Split Pea Root Vegetable Soup, 67
　Sweet Potato Tabbouleh, 146
　Wheat Berry Harvest Salad, 76
Dates
　Coconut Maple Truffles, 167
Desserts
　Almond Quinoa Pudding, 69
　Chocolate Cashew Bars, 19
　Chocolate Mint Mousse, 129
　Chocolate Sesame Oat Bites, 166
　Coconut Maple Truffles, 167
　Lemon Mascarpone Cream Sauce with Strawberries, 39
　Orange Pots de Crème, 168
　Sesame Brown Rice Treats, 59
Dips and spreads
　Classic Hummus, 89
　Mediterranean Layered Dip, 49
　Roasted Red Pepper Spread, 109
Dressings
　Creamy Peanut Dressing, 176
　Hoisin Dressing and Marinade, 175
　Simple Herbed Balsamic Dressing, 174

E

Eggs
　Banana Baked Oatmeal, 65
　Brussels Sprout Egg Skillet, 143
　Canadian Bacon and Goat Cheese Egg Muffins, 142
　Crêpes with Raspberries, 85
　Ham and Cheese Breakfast Casserole, 141
　Lemon Pancakes, 138

Mediterranean Breakfast Wraps, 75
Orange Pots de Crème, 168
Pumpkin Sausage Egg Casserole, 55
Savory Farro Breakfast Bowl, 140
Strawberry French Toast Casserole, 115
Sweet Potato Spinach Frittata, 105
Veggie and Feta Egg Sandwich, 135
Western Omelet Sandwiches, 15
White Bean Breakfast Burritos, 125
Equipment, 4

F

Farro
Balsamic-Marinated Halibut with Farro, 152
Mediterranean Turkey Bowls, 66
Savory Farro Breakfast Bowl, 140
Sheet-Pan Sausage and Peppers, 96
Fish
Baked Lemon Garlic Trout with Potato Wedges, 97
Balsamic-Marinated Halibut with Farro, 152
Cashew-Crusted Halibut with Brown Rice, 88
Hoisin Salmon with Bok Choy, 151
Honey Sesame Salmon with Squash, 68
Pesto Tilapia Vegetable Packets, 58
Salmon, Potato, and French Bean Sheet-Pan Bake, 28
Fluffy Buttermilk Pancakes, 35
Food storage
containers, 5–6
guidelines, 6–8
refrigerator/freezer storage chart, 9
Freezer storage chart, 9
French beans. See Green beans

G

Garam Masala Chicken Thighs with Broccoli, 57
Glass containers, 6
Gluten-free
All-Purpose Spice Rub, 173
Almond Quinoa Pudding, 69
Apple Pie Overnight Oats, 25
Avocado Cherry Kale Smoothie, 160
Bacon Breakfast Cassoulet, 45
Baked Lemon Garlic Trout with Potato Wedges, 97
Balsamic-Marinated Halibut with Farro, 152
Banana Baked Oatmeal, 65
Beet and Berry Smoothie, 119
Black Bean Chili Quesadillas, 46
Brussels Sprout Egg Skillet, 143
Canadian Bacon and Goat Cheese Egg Muffins, 142
Cashew-Crusted Halibut with Brown Rice, 88
Cheesy Chicken Broccoli Casserole, 18
Chicken Caprese Salad, 148
Chicken Cobb Salad, 26
Chicken Spinach Chowder, 126
Chickpea Root Vegetable Curry, 150
Chocolate Cashew Bars, 19
Chocolate Hazelnut Steel-Cut Oats, 134
Chocolate Mint Mousse, 129
Chocolate Sesame Oat Bites, 166
Classic Hummus, 89
Coconut Maple Truffles, 167
Creamy Curry Chicken and Rice, 98
Creamy Potato Leek Soup, 56
Crispy Chili Kale Chips, 99
Crunchy Lettuce Cajun Coleslaw Wraps, 16
Garam Masala Chicken Thighs with Broccoli, 57
Golden Roasted Chickpeas, 165
Granola Muesli, 95
Green Chia Smoothie, 161
Ham and Cheese Breakfast Casserole, 141
Honey Sesame Salmon with Squash, 68
Korean-Style Beef with Brown Rice, 107
Lemon Mascarpone Cream Sauce with Strawberries, 39
Marinated Flank Steak with Pico de Gallo, 38
Mocha Protein Smoothie, 162
Noodle Bowls with Peanut Sauce, 149
Oktoberfest Soup, 117
Orange Pots de Crème, 168
Pecan-Crusted Pork Chops with Mashed Potatoes, 77
Pesto Tilapia Vegetable Packets, 58
Pico de Gallo, 179
Pomegranate Blueberry Smoothie, 163
Pumpkin Pie Tofu "Milkshake," 79
Pumpkin Sausage Egg Casserole, 55
Quinoa Pecan Granola, 137

Gluten-free (*continued*)
- Roasted Tofu Acorn Squash Bake, 127
- Salad Bowls with Tzatziki Sauce, 106
- Salmon, Potato, and French Bean Sheet-Pan Bake, 28
- Sesame Brown Rice Treats, 59
- Shawarma Chicken with Root Vegetables, 37
- Shawarma-Rubbed Pork Sheet-Pan Dinner, 155
- Shawarma Spice Blend, 172
- Sheet-Pan Chicken Parmesan, 78
- Sheet-Pan Country Breakfast, 139
- Sheet-Pan Sausage and Peppers, 96
- Simple Herbed Balsamic Dressing, 174
- Simple Slow Cooker Chicken Stew, 87
- Slow Cooker Chipotle Chili, 128
- Slow Cooker Tomato and Beef Stew, 47
- Southwest Broccoli Salad, 147
- Spice-Rubbed Pork Tenderloin, 48
- Spicy Vegetarian Chili, 17
- Split Pea Root Vegetable Soup, 67
- Sweet Potato Spinach Frittata, 105
- Traditional Basil Pesto, 177
- Turkey Taco Stuffed Baked Potatoes, 154
- Tzatziki Sauce, 178

Golden Roasted Chickpeas, 165

Granola
- Granola Muesli, 95
- Quinoa Pecan Granola, 137

Green beans
- Balsamic-Marinated Halibut with Farro, 152
- Cashew-Crusted Halibut with Brown Rice, 88
- Chicken Spinach Chowder, 126
- Salmon, Potato, and French Bean Sheet-Pan Bake, 28
- Veggie and Feta Egg Sandwich, 135

Green Chia Smoothie, 161

H

Halibut
- Balsamic-Marinated Halibut with Farro, 152
- Cashew-Crusted Halibut with Brown Rice, 88

Ham
- Canadian Bacon and Goat Cheese Egg Muffins, 142
- Ham and Cheese Breakfast Casserole, 141
- Western Omelet Sandwiches, 15

Hoisin Dressing and Marinade, 175
Hoisin Salmon with Bok Choy, 151
Honey Sesame Salmon with Squash, 68

K

Kale
- Avocado Cherry Kale Smoothie, 160
- Bacon Breakfast Cassoulet, 45
- Beet and Berry Smoothie, 119
- Crispy Chili Kale Chips, 99
- Ham and Cheese Breakfast Casserole, 141
- Pomegranate Blueberry Smoothie, 163

Korean-Style Beef with Brown Rice, 107

L

Labeling, 7
Lamb Burgers with Tzatziki Sauce, 118
Leek Potato Soup, Creamy, 56

Lemons
- Baked Lemon Garlic Trout with Potato Wedges, 97
- Lemon Mascarpone Cream Sauce with Strawberries, 39
- Lemon Pancakes, 138

Lettuce
- Chicken Caprese Salad, 148
- Chicken Cobb Salad, 26
- Crunchy Lettuce Cajun Coleslaw Wraps, 16
- Lamb Burgers with Tzatziki Sauce, 118

M

Mangos
- Green Chia Smoothie, 161

Marinades
- Hoisin Dressing and Marinade, 175

Marinated Flank Steak with Pico de Gallo, 38

Marshmallows
- Sesame Brown Rice Treats, 59

Mascarpone Lemon Cream Sauce with Strawberries, 39

Mason jars, 6

Meal prepping
- benefits of, 2–3
- week 1, 11–19
- week 2, 21–29
- week 3, 31–39
- week 4, 41–49
- week 5, 51–59
- week 6, 61–69

week 7, 71–79
week 8, 81–89
week 9, 91–99
week 10, 101–109
week 11, 111–119
week 12, 121–129
Mediterranean Breakfast Wraps, 75
Mediterranean Layered Dip, 49
Mediterranean Turkey Bowls, 66
Mocha Protein Smoothie, 162
Mushrooms
  Ham and Cheese Breakfast Casserole, 141

N

Noodles. *See also* Pasta
  Noodle Bowls with Peanut Sauce, 149
  Paprika Chicken with Butter Noodles, 108
Nut-free
  All-Purpose Spice Rub, 173
  Apple Pie Overnight Oats, 25
  Avocado Cherry Kale Smoothie, 160
  Bacon Breakfast Cassoulet, 45
  Baked Lemon Garlic Trout with Potato Wedges, 97
  Balsamic-Marinated Halibut with Farro, 152
  Banana Baked Oatmeal, 65
  Beef-Stuffed Squash, 156
  Black Bean Chili Quesadillas, 46
  Brussels Sprout Egg Skillet, 143
  Canadian Bacon and Goat Cheese Egg Muffins, 142
  Cheesy Chicken Broccoli Casserole, 18
  Chicken Caprese Salad, 148
  Chicken Cobb Salad, 26
  Chicken Spinach Chowder, 126
  Chickpea Root Vegetable Curry, 150
  Chickpea Salad Pinwheels, 164
  Chocolate Mint Mousse, 129
  Classic Hummus, 89
  Coconut Maple Truffles, 167
  Creamy Curry Chicken and Rice, 98
  Creamy Potato Leek Soup, 56
  Crêpes with Raspberries, 85
  Crispy Chili Kale Chips, 99
  Crunchy Lettuce Cajun Coleslaw Wraps, 16
  Fluffy Buttermilk Pancakes, 35
  Garam Masala Chicken Thighs with Broccoli, 57
  Golden Roasted Chickpeas, 165
  Green Chia Smoothie, 161
  Ham and Cheese Breakfast Casserole, 141
  Hoisin Dressing and Marinade, 175
  Hoisin Salmon with Bok Choy, 151
  Honey Sesame Salmon with Squash, 68
  Korean-Style Beef with Brown Rice, 107
  Lamb Burgers with Tzatziki Sauce, 118
  Lemon Mascarpone Cream Sauce with Strawberries, 39
  Lemon Pancakes, 138
  Marinated Flank Steak with Pico de Gallo, 38
  Mediterranean Breakfast Wraps, 75
  Mediterranean Layered Dip, 49
  Mediterranean Turkey Bowls, 66
  Oktoberfest Soup, 117
  Orange Pots de Crème, 168
  Paprika Chicken with Butter Noodles, 108
  Pico de Gallo, 179
  Pomegranate Blueberry Smoothie, 163
  Pumpkin Pie Tofu "Milkshake," 79
  Pumpkin Sausage Egg Casserole, 55
  Roasted Tofu Acorn Squash Bake, 127
  Salad Bowls with Tzatziki Sauce, 106
  Salmon, Potato, and French Bean Sheet-Pan Bake, 28
  Savory Farro Breakfast Bowl, 140
  Sesame Brown Rice Treats, 59
  Sesame Zoodles with Summer Vegetables, 36
  Shawarma Chicken with Root Vegetables, 37
  Shawarma-Rubbed Pork Sheet-Pan Dinner, 155
  Shawarma Spice Blend, 172
  Sheet-Pan Beef Fajitas, 157
  Sheet-Pan Chicken Parmesan, 78
  Sheet-Pan Country Breakfast, 139
  Sheet-Pan Sausage and Peppers, 96
  Simple Herbed Balsamic Dressing, 174
  Simple Slow Cooker Chicken Stew, 87
  Slow Cooker Chipotle Chili, 128
  Slow Cooker Tomato and Beef Stew, 47
  Southwest Broccoli Salad, 147
  Spaghetti Bolognese, 27
  Spice-Rubbed Pork Tenderloin, 48

Nut-free (*continued*)
- Spicy Vegetarian Chili, 17
- Spinach Mac and Cheese, 86
- Split Pea Root Vegetable Soup, 67
- Strawberry French Toast Casserole, 115
- Sweet Potato Spinach Frittata, 105
- Sweet Potato Tabbouleh, 146
- Turkey Taco Stuffed Baked Potatoes, 154
- Tzatziki Sauce, 178
- Veggie and Feta Egg Sandwich, 135
- Western Omelet Sandwiches, 15
- White Bean Breakfast Burritos, 125

Nuts
- Almond Quinoa Pudding, 69
- Banana Walnut Couscous, 136
- Cashew-Crusted Halibut with Brown Rice, 88
- Chocolate Cashew Bars, 19
- Chocolate Hazelnut Steel-Cut Oats, 134
- Pecan-Crusted Pork Chops with Mashed Potatoes, 77
- Quinoa Pecan Granola, 137
- Roasted Red Pepper Spread, 109
- Spicy Snack Mix, 29
- Traditional Basil Pesto, 177
- Wheat Berry Harvest Salad, 76

O

Oats
- Apple Pie Overnight Oats, 25
- Banana Baked Oatmeal, 65
- Chocolate Cashew Bars, 19
- Chocolate Hazelnut Steel-Cut Oats, 134
- Chocolate Sesame Oat Bites, 166
- Coconut Maple Truffles, 167
- Peanut Butter Honey Fruit Wrap, 169
- Quinoa Pecan Granola, 137

Oktoberfest Soup, 117

Olives
- Antipasto Couscous Salad, 116

Orange Pots de Crème, 168

P

Pantry staples, 3–4

Paprika Chicken with Butter Noodles, 108

Parsnips
- Chickpea Root Vegetable Curry, 150
- Shawarma Chicken with Root Vegetables, 37
- Sheet-Pan Chicken Parmesan, 78

Pasta
- Chicken Pesto Penne, 153
- Sesame Zoodles with Summer Vegetables, 36
- Spaghetti Bolognese, 27
- Spinach Mac and Cheese, 86

Peanut butter
- Chocolate Sesame Oat Bites, 166
- Creamy Peanut Dressing, 176
- Peanut Butter Honey Fruit Wrap, 169

Peas
- Noodle Bowls with Peanut Sauce, 149
- Slow Cooker Tomato and Beef Stew, 47

Pecan-Crusted Pork Chops with Mashed Potatoes, 77

Peppers
- Antipasto Couscous Salad, 116
- Beef-Stuffed Squash, 156
- Canadian Bacon and Goat Cheese Egg Muffins, 142
- Korean-Style Beef with Brown Rice, 107
- Mediterranean Turkey Bowls, 66
- Noodle Bowls with Peanut Sauce, 149
- Pico de Gallo, 179
- Pumpkin Sausage Egg Casserole, 55
- Roasted Red Pepper Spread, 109
- Roasted Tofu Acorn Squash Bake, 127
- Shawarma-Rubbed Pork Sheet-Pan Dinner, 155
- Sheet-Pan Beef Fajitas, 157
- Sheet-Pan Country Breakfast, 139
- Sheet-Pan Sausage and Peppers, 96
- Southwest Broccoli Salad, 147
- Spice-Rubbed Pork Tenderloin, 48
- Spicy Vegetarian Chili, 17
- Sweet Potato Tabbouleh, 146
- Veggie and Feta Egg Sandwich, 135
- Western Omelet Sandwiches, 15
- White Bean Breakfast Burritos, 125

Pesto
- Chicken Pesto Penne, 153
- Pesto Tilapia Vegetable Packets, 58
- Traditional Basil Pesto, 177

Pico de Gallo, 179

Plastic containers, 5

Pomegranate Blueberry Smoothie, 163

Pork. *See also* Bacon; Ham; Sausage

Pecan-Crusted Pork Chops with Mashed Potatoes, 77
Shawarma-Rubbed Pork Sheet-Pan Dinner, 155
Spice-Rubbed Pork Tenderloin, 48

Potatoes. *See also* Sweet potatoes
Bacon Breakfast Cassoulet, 45
Baked Lemon Garlic Trout with Potato Wedges, 97
Chicken Spinach Chowder, 126
Creamy Potato Leek Soup, 56
Oktoberfest Soup, 117
Pecan-Crusted Pork Chops with Mashed Potatoes, 77
Salmon, Potato, and French Bean Sheet-Pan Bake, 28
Sheet-Pan Country Breakfast, 139
Simple Slow Cooker Chicken Stew, 87
Slow Cooker Tomato and Beef Stew, 47

Pretzels
Spicy Snack Mix, 29

Prosciutto
Antipasto Couscous Salad, 116

Pumpkin Pie Tofu "Milkshake," 79

Pumpkin Sausage Egg Casserole, 55

Q

Quinoa
Almond Quinoa Pudding, 69
Quinoa Pecan Granola, 137

R

Recipes, about, 8
Refrigerator storage chart, 9
Reheating, 8
Rice

Cashew-Crusted Halibut with Brown Rice, 88
Cheesy Chicken Broccoli Casserole, 18
Chickpea Root Vegetable Curry, 150
Creamy Curry Chicken and Rice, 98
Garam Masala Chicken Thighs with Broccoli, 57
Hoisin Salmon with Bok Choy, 151
Korean-Style Beef with Brown Rice, 107
Marinated Flank Steak with Pico de Gallo, 38
Roasted Red Pepper Spread, 109
Roasted Tofu Acorn Squash Bake, 127

S

Salads. *See also* Bowls
Antipasto Couscous Salad, 116
Chicken Caprese Salad, 148
Chicken Cobb Salad, 26
Salad Bowls with Tzatziki Sauce, 106
Southwest Broccoli Salad, 147
Sweet Potato Tabbouleh, 146
Wheat Berry Harvest Salad, 76

Salami
Antipasto Couscous Salad, 116

Salmon
Hoisin Salmon with Bok Choy, 151
Honey Sesame Salmon with Squash, 68
Salmon, Potato, and French Bean Sheet-Pan Bake, 28

Salsa
Marinated Flank Steak with Pico de Gallo, 38

Mediterranean Layered Dip, 49
Pico de Gallo, 179
Sheet-Pan Beef Fajitas, 157
Turkey Taco Stuffed Baked Potatoes, 154

Sandwiches. *See also* Wraps
Lamb Burgers with Tzatziki Sauce, 118
Veggie and Feta Egg Sandwich, 135
Western Omelet Sandwiches, 15

Sauces. *See also* Dressings
Pico de Gallo, 179
Traditional Basil Pesto, 177
Tzatziki Sauce, 178

Sausage
Oktoberfest Soup, 117
Pumpkin Sausage Egg Casserole, 55
Sheet-Pan Country Breakfast, 139
Sheet-Pan Sausage and Peppers, 96

Savory Farro Breakfast Bowl, 140

Sesame Brown Rice Treats, 59

Sesame Zoodles with Summer Vegetables, 36

Shawarma Chicken with Root Vegetables, 37

Shawarma-Rubbed Pork Sheet-Pan Dinner, 155

Shawarma Spice Blend, 172

Sheet-Pan Beef Fajitas, 157

Sheet-Pan Chicken Parmesan, 78

Sheet-Pan Country Breakfast, 139

Sheet-Pan Sausage and Peppers, 96

Simple Herbed Balsamic Dressing, 174

INDEX 189

Simple Slow Cooker
Chicken Stew, 87
Slow Cooker Chipotle Chili, 128
Slow Cooker Tomato and
Beef Stew, 47
Smoothies and shakes
Avocado Cherry Kale
Smoothie, 160
Beet and Berry Smoothie, 119
Green Chia Smoothie, 161
Mocha Protein Smoothie, 162
Pomegranate Blueberry
Smoothie, 163
Pumpkin Pie Tofu
"Milkshake," 79
Snacks
Chocolate Cashew Bars, 19
Chocolate Sesame
Oat Bites, 166
Classic Hummus, 89
Crispy Chili Kale Chips, 99
Golden Roasted
Chickpeas, 165
Mediterranean
Layered Dip, 49
Peanut Butter Honey
Fruit Wrap, 169
Roasted Red Pepper
Spread, 109
Sesame Brown Rice Treats, 59
Spicy Snack Mix, 29
Soups. See also Chilis; Stews
Chicken Spinach
Chowder, 126
Creamy Potato Leek Soup, 56
Oktoberfest Soup, 117
Split Pea Root Vegetable
Soup, 67
Sour cream
Mediterranean
Layered Dip, 49
Southwest Broccoli Salad, 147

Soy crumbles
Crunchy Lettuce Cajun
Coleslaw Wraps, 16
Spaghetti Bolognese, 27
Spice blends
All-Purpose Spice Rub, 173
Shawarma Spice Blend, 172
Spice-Rubbed Pork
Tenderloin, 48
Spicy Snack Mix, 29
Spicy Vegetarian Chili, 17
Spinach
Chicken Pesto Penne, 153
Chicken Spinach
Chowder, 126
Green Chia Smoothie, 161
Mediterranean Breakfast
Wraps, 75
Pumpkin Sausage Egg
Casserole, 55
Spinach Mac and Cheese, 86
Sweet Potato Spinach
Frittata, 105
Spinach Mac and Cheese, 86
Split Pea Root Vegetable
Soup, 67
Squash. See also Zucchini
Beef-Stuffed Squash, 156
Honey Sesame Salmon
with Squash, 68
Roasted Tofu Acorn
Squash Bake, 127
Stainless steel containers, 6
Stews. See also Chilis
Chickpea Root Vegetable
Curry, 150
Simple Slow Cooker
Chicken Stew, 87
Slow Cooker Tomato
and Beef Stew, 47
Storage containers, 5–6
Strawberry French Toast
Casserole, 115
Sunflower seeds
Granola Muesli, 95

Roasted Tofu Acorn
Squash Bake, 127
Sweet potatoes
Chickpea Root Vegetable
Curry, 150
Shawarma Chicken with
Root Vegetables, 37
Sheet-Pan Country
Breakfast, 139
Sweet Potato Spinach
Frittata, 105
Sweet Potato Tabbouleh, 146
Turkey Taco Stuffed
Baked Potatoes, 154
Wheat Berry Harvest Salad, 76

T

Tahini
Classic Hummus, 89
Thawing, 8
Tilapia Vegetable Packets,
Pesto, 58
Tofu
Pumpkin Pie Tofu
"Milkshake," 79
Roasted Tofu Acorn
Squash Bake, 127
Tomatoes
Antipasto Couscous
Salad, 116
Chicken Caprese Salad, 148
Chicken Cobb Salad, 26
Creamy Curry Chicken
and Rice, 98
Mediterranean Breakfast
Wraps, 75
Pico de Gallo, 179
Salad Bowls with Tzatziki
Sauce, 106
Savory Farro Breakfast
Bowl, 140
Slow Cooker Chipotle
Chili, 128

Slow Cooker Tomato
    and Beef Stew, 47
Spaghetti Bolognese, 27
Spicy Vegetarian Chili, 17
Tortillas
  Black Bean Chili
      Quesadillas, 46
  Chickpea Salad
      Pinwheels, 164
  Mediterranean Breakfast
      Wraps, 75
  Peanut Butter Honey
      Fruit Wrap, 169
  Sheet-Pan Beef Fajitas, 157
  White Bean Breakfast
      Burritos, 125
Traditional Basil Pesto, 177
Trout, Baked Lemon Garlic,
    with Potato Wedges, 97
Turkey
  Mediterranean Turkey
      Bowls, 66
  Slow Cooker Chipotle
      Chili, 128
  Turkey Taco Stuffed
      Baked Potatoes, 154
Tzatziki Sauce, 178

V

Vegan
  All-Purpose Spice Rub, 173
  Almond Quinoa Pudding, 69
  Beet and Berry Smoothie, 119
  Chocolate Sesame
      Oat Bites, 166
  Classic Hummus, 89
  Coconut Maple Truffles, 167
  Creamy Peanut Dressing, 176
  Crispy Chili Kale Chips, 99
  Golden Roasted
      Chickpeas, 165
  Green Chia Smoothie, 161
  Hoisin Dressing and
      Marinade, 175
  Pico de Gallo, 179

Pomegranate Blueberry
    Smoothie, 163
Quinoa Pecan Granola, 137
Roasted Tofu Acorn
    Squash Bake, 127
Sesame Zoodles with
    Summer Vegetables, 36
Shawarma Spice Blend, 172
Simple Herbed Balsamic
    Dressing, 174
Spicy Snack Mix, 29
Spicy Vegetarian Chili, 17
Sweet Potato Tabbouleh, 146
Wheat Berry Harvest Salad, 76
Vegetarian. *See also* Vegan
  Apple Pie Overnight Oats, 25
  Avocado Cherry Kale
      Smoothie, 160
  Banana Baked Oatmeal, 65
  Banana Walnut Couscous, 136
  Black Bean Chili
      Quesadillas, 46
  Chickpea Root Vegetable
      Curry, 150
  Chickpea Salad
      Pinwheels, 164
  Chocolate Cashew Bars, 19
  Chocolate Hazelnut
      Steel-Cut Oats, 134
  Chocolate Mint Mousse, 129
  Creamy Potato Leek Soup, 56
  Crêpes with Raspberries, 85
  Crunchy Lettuce Cajun
      Coleslaw Wraps, 16
  Fluffy Buttermilk Pancakes, 35
  Granola Muesli, 95
  Lemon Mascarpone
      Cream Sauce with
      Strawberries, 39
  Lemon Pancakes, 138
  Mediterranean Breakfast
      Wraps, 75
  Mediterranean
      Layered Dip, 49
  Mocha Protein Smoothie, 162

  Noodle Bowls with
      Peanut Sauce, 149
  Orange Pots de Crème, 168
  Peanut Butter Honey
      Fruit Wrap, 169
  Pumpkin Pie Tofu
      "Milkshake," 79
  Savory Farro Breakfast
      Bowl, 140
  Sesame Brown Rice Treats,
      59
  Spinach Mac and Cheese, 86
  Strawberry French Toast
      Casserole, 115
  Sweet Potato Spinach
      Frittata, 105
  Traditional Basil Pesto, 177
  Tzatziki Sauce, 178
  Veggie and Feta Egg
      Sandwich, 135
  White Bean Breakfast
      Burritos, 125
Veggie and Feta Egg
    Sandwich, 135

W

Western Omelet Sandwiches,
    15
Wheat Berry Harvest Salad, 76
White Bean Breakfast
    Burritos, 125
Wraps
  Black Bean Chili
      Quesadillas, 46
  Chickpea Salad
      Pinwheels, 164
  Crunchy Lettuce Cajun
      Coleslaw Wraps, 16
  Mediterranean Breakfast
      Wraps, 75
  Peanut Butter Honey
      Fruit Wrap, 169
  Sheet-Pan Beef Fajitas, 157
  White Bean Breakfast
      Burritos, 125

Y

Yogurt
- Apple Pie Overnight Oats, 25
- Granola Muesli, 95
- Lemon Mascarpone Cream Sauce with Strawberries, 39

Mocha Protein Smoothie, 162
Tzatziki Sauce, 178

Z

Zucchini
- Canadian Bacon and Goat Cheese Egg Muffins, 142

Sesame Zoodles with Summer Vegetables, 36
Shawarma-Rubbed Pork Sheet-Pan Dinner, 155
Spice-Rubbed Pork Tenderloin, 48

Acknowledgments

I am grateful to the Callisto Media team for their incredible hard work and for giving me the opportunity to work on more than 30 books with them over the years. They have helped me become a better writer.

Thank you to all the chefs, suppliers, farmers, and home cooks over the last 30 years who have contributed to my knowledge of food and imparted their passion for exceptional ingredients and wonderful recipes.

About the Author

MICHELLE ANDERSON is the author and ghostwriter of more than 35 cookbooks focused on healthy diets and delicious food. She worked as a professional chef for more than 25 years, honing her craft overseas in North Africa and all over Ontario, Canada, in fine dining restaurants. She also worked as a corporate executive chef for Rational Canada for four years, collaborating with her international counterparts and consulting in kitchens all over Southern Ontario and in the United States. Previously, Michelle ran her own catering company and personal chef business and was a wedding cake designer. Her focus was on food as medicine and using wholesome, quality field-to-fork ingredients in vibrant, visually impactful dishes. Michelle lives in Temiskaming Shores, Ontario, Canada, with her husband, two sons, two Newfoundland dogs, and three cats.

www.ingramcontent.com/pod-product-compliance
Lightning Source LLC
Chambersburg PA
CBHW061418090426
42743CB00023B/3489